Level F

TEST BEST®

for Test Prep

Strategies for
- *Reading*
- *Vocabulary*
- *Math*
- *Listening*
- *Language*

STECK-VAUGHN
BERRENT
A Harcourt Company

www.steck-vaughn.com

Test Best® for Test Prep
Level F

Contents

Unit 1	Reading: Test-Taking Strategies	3
Unit 2	Reading Comprehension: Modeled Instruction	6
Unit 3	Reading Comprehension	31
Unit 4	Reading Vocabulary	47
Unit 5	Math: Problem-Solving Strategies	53
Unit 6	Math Problem Solving	56
Unit 7	Listening	79
Unit 8	Language	83
Unit 9	Practice Test 1: Reading Comprehension	95
Unit 10	Practice Test 2: Reading Vocabulary	103
Unit 11	Practice Test 3: Math	106
Unit 12	Practice Test 4: Listening	118
Unit 13	Practice Test 5: Language	120
Answer Sheet		127

Credits

Project Editor: Amy Losi
Cover Design: Steven Coleman

Test Best® is a registered trademark of Steck-Vaughn Company.

Test Best for Test Prep — Level F

ISBN 0-8172-5829-9

Copyright © 1999 Steck-Vaughn Company.

All rights reserved. No part of this book may be reproduced or utilized in any form or by any means, electronic, or mechanical, including photocopying, recording, or by any information storage and retrieval system, without permission in writing from the publisher. Inquiries should be addressed to : Copyright Permissions, Steck-Vaughn Company, P. O. Box 26015, Austin, TX 78755. Printed in the United States of America.

Published by © Steck-Vaughn/Berrent Publications, a division of Steck-Vaughn Company.

6 7 8 9   DBH   03 02 01

UNIT ONE
Reading: Test-Taking Strategies

The following strategies will help you do your best on standardized reading tests. These three strategies will assist you in organizing the information needed to successfully answer the questions.

STRATEGY 1

The CHECK AND SEE Strategy

This strategy can be used when a question asks for a fact from the story. The answer to the question is right there in the story. It is not hidden. Some of the same words may be in the story and in the question.

 Check and See will help you answer *remembering information* questions.

This is the Check and See Strategy

1. **READ: Read** the question.

2. **FIND: Find** the words you need in the story.

3. **DECIDE: Decide** which strategy to use.
   Check and See: Put a **check** next to the sentence where you can **see** the words you need to answer the question.

4. **ANSWER:** Choose the best **answer**.

STRATEGY 2

The PUZZLE PIECE Strategy

This strategy can be used when a question asks you what something means. Sometimes there does not seem to be an answer. It is not stated in the story.

Puzzle Piece is the strategy to use when you must fit facts together to get the answer. This is like putting a puzzle together. Puzzles are made up of many pieces. You cannot look at one piece and know what the picture is. Only when you put the pieces together can you see the whole picture.

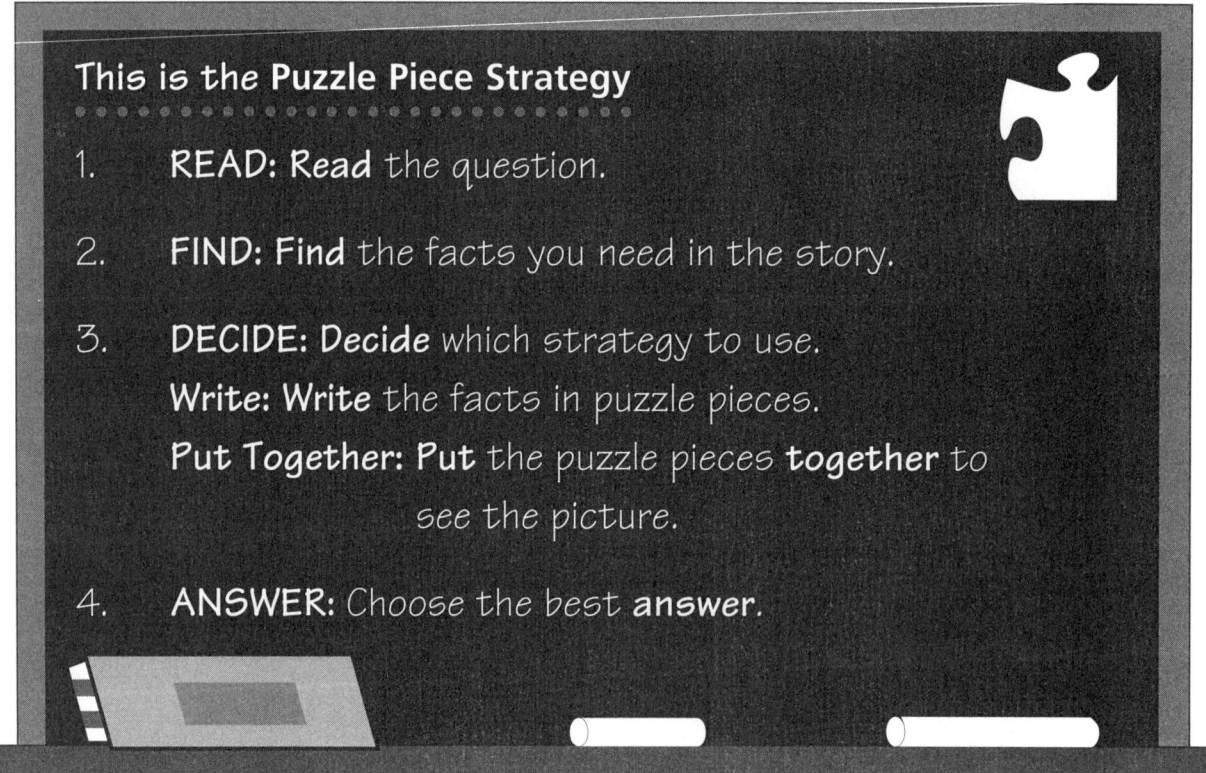

This is the Puzzle Piece Strategy

1. READ: **Read** the question.

2. FIND: **Find** the facts you need in the story.

3. DECIDE: **Decide** which strategy to use.
   Write: **Write** the facts in puzzle pieces.
   Put Together: **Put** the puzzle pieces **together** to see the picture.

4. ANSWER: Choose the best **answer**.

STRATEGY 3

The WHAT LIGHTS UP Strategy

This is another strategy you can use when an answer is not in the story. To answer the question you need to add your own ideas to the story. This added information can come from your own experiences.

What Lights Up can help you see if something is true, real, useful, or a fact. It can help you see what would happen if the story had a different ending.

You can use the **What Lights Up Strategy** to answer the hardest type of question. This is when you are asked to read and think of your own ideas. These questions are called *evaluating* and extending meaning questions.

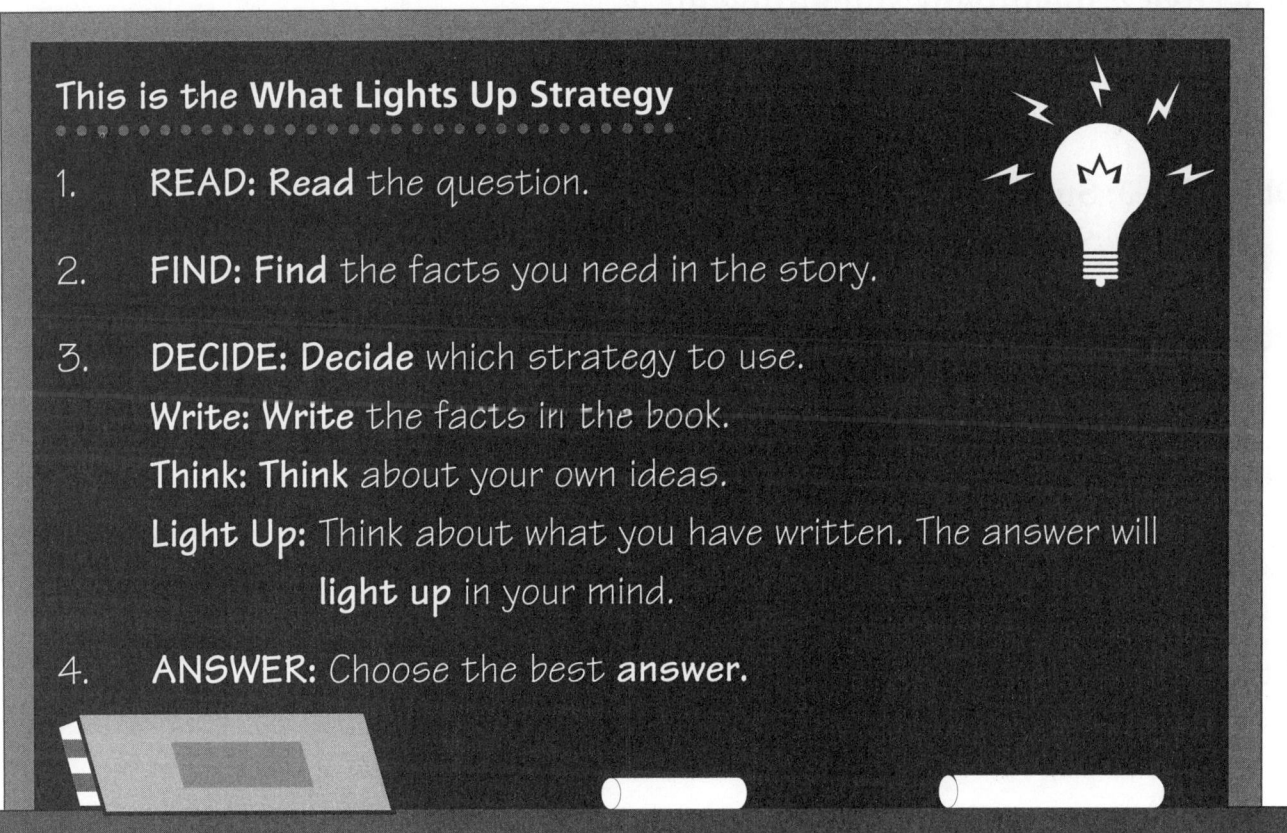

This is the What Lights Up Strategy

1. READ: **Read** the question.
2. FIND: **Find** the facts you need in the story.
3. DECIDE: **Decide** which strategy to use.
   Write: **Write** the facts in the book.
   Think: **Think** about your own ideas.
   Light Up: Think about what you have written. The answer will **light up** in your mind.
4. ANSWER: Choose the best **answer**.

UNIT TWO
Reading Comprehension
Modeled Instruction

Specific Objectives

Objective 1: Determining word meanings
Prefixes and suffixes, context clues, technical words, and words with multiple meanings

Objective 2: Identifying supporting ideas
Recalling facts and details, sequential order, following directions, and describing settings

Objective 3: Summarizing main ideas
Stated and implied main ideas, and identifying summaries

Objective 4: Perceiving relationships and recognizing outcomes
Cause-and-effect and making predictions

Objective 5: Making inferences and generalizations
Interpreting graphs and diagrams, inferring information, drawing conclusions, making judgments, and evaluating plot

Objective 6: Recognizing points of view, facts, and opinions
Author's purpose, persuasive language, and discerning facts and points of view

Modeled Instruction

Objective 1: Determining Word Meanings

Prefixes and suffixes are parts of some words. A *prefix* **appears at the beginning of a word. A** *suffix* **appears at the end of a word. Both prefixes and suffixes affect the meaning of the word. Readers can use them to help figure out the meaning of a word.**

Tom's grandfather came for the weekend. He played in the sandbox and on the swings, and his team won kickball in the park. Tom and his friends loved it, but Tom's mother thought her father was acting childish.

1. **In this paragraph, the word childish means —**

   A like a child.

   B in a cold, unfriendly manner.

   C in the best interests of the children.

   D like an invalid.

   Hint: The suffix "-ish" means like.

Everyone in the class agreed that they should plant flowers around the flagpole. They wanted to beautify the school grounds.

2. **In this paragraph, the word beautify means —**

   F to take something that is beautiful.

   G to explain what beautiful means.

   H to make something beautiful.

   J the same thing as pretty.

   Hint: The suffix "-fy" means to make.

Not only was the kitten inside a carrying case, but it was also inside the airliner with all the other cargo. The cat wanted its freedom!

3. **In this paragraph, the word freedom means —**

   A ability to move without restraint.

   B cat food.

   C home.

   D ability to choose actions.

   Hint: The suffix "-dom" means state of.

Answers
1 Ⓐ Ⓑ Ⓒ Ⓓ   2 Ⓕ Ⓖ Ⓗ Ⓙ   3 Ⓐ Ⓑ Ⓒ Ⓓ

Objective 1: Determining Word Meanings

Sometimes we can figure out the meaning of a new or difficult word by using the words around it as clues.

Someday, a computer in your car may tell you where you're going. An arrow will move across a map, showing where the car is. You won't see many of these computers in cars soon, however. Their cost is prohibitive.

4 **In this paragraph, the word prohibitive means —**

    F lost all the time.

    G too high.

    H cheap.

    J fast.

Hint: You get a clue about what the word prohibitive *means by reading sentences 3 and 4.*

Eli Whitney was ingenious. Not only did he invent the cotton gin, but he also produced the first working model of it in only ten days.

5 **In this paragraph, the word ingenious means —**

    A unhappily married.

    B a cloth maker.

    C born in the South.

    D very clever.

Hint: Check each choice to see which one fits best.

The king cobra is a very dangerous snake. Its bite can kill an elephant in three hours. Most animals attack only when threatened. But the king cobra will attack without being provoked.

6 **What might happen if you provoked someone?**

_____

_____

_____

_____

Hint: You get a clue about what the word provoked *means by reading sentences 3 and 4.*

Answers
4 Ⓕ Ⓖ Ⓗ Ⓙ   5 Ⓐ Ⓑ Ⓒ Ⓓ

Objective 1: Determining Word Meanings

Specialized or technical words are words used in specific subjects, such as science and social studies. Readers can use all the other information in the text to help determine the meaning of these words.

The mummies of Egypt are very old. So people assume the Egyptians had special ways of embalming. Actually, it was the dry air that helped preserve their dead.

7 In this paragraph, the word embalming means —

F making pyramids.

G keeping the dead from decaying.

H keeping things alive.

J dealing with heat.

Hint: Embalming is a technical word. You get a clue about what it means by reading the entire paragraph.

Galileo was a famous scientist, but he did not invent the telescope. He did improve the device. He was the first person to use a telescope to look at the stars.

8 In this paragraph, the word telescope means —

A a map of the sea.

B an instrument to magnify.

C a listening device.

D a camera.

Hint: Telescope is a technical word. You get a clue about what it means by reading about what it was used for.

On the ocean, distance is measured in nautical miles. This kind of mile is about 800 feet longer than the mile used for measuring land.

9 In this paragraph, the word nautical means —

F sea.

G whale.

H shorter.

J probable.

Hint: The word nautical is a technical term. You get a clue about what it means by reading the entire paragraph.

Some owls have long, vicious talons. They use them to catch mice to eat. They also use them to defend their nests against enemies.

10 What are talons?

_____

_____

_____

_____

Hint: The word talons is a technical word. You get a clue about what it means by reading what they are used for.

Answers
7 F G H J   8 A B C D   9 F G H J

9

Objective 2: Identifying Supporting Ideas

Some facts and details are important. By noticing and remembering those that support the main idea or conclusion, you will better understand what the passage is about.

Toronto has the world's largest shopping mall under the ground. It has more than 1,000 shops and services. They are joined by miles of tunnels and sidewalks. These tunnels and sidewalks also join 35 high-rise buildings. To get to the underground mall, shoppers go in one of the buildings and ride the elevator down. People can also take the subway to other parts of the city. The city-under-the-city is always a pleasant place to walk. That's because the temperature is controlled. Outside, winter may be cold or summer may be hot. But deep down in the mall, the temperature stays the same all year round.

1. In the shopping mall, there are more than 1,000 —

    A tunnels and sidewalks.

    B shops and services.

    C business workers.

    D underground trains.

    Hint: This fact is right in the passage.

2. To get from one part of the mall to another, people take —

    F tunnels.

    G skywalks.

    H subways.

    J elevators.

    Hint: Look for the fact in the selection.

3. Where is the largest underground mall located?

    _____
    _____
    _____
    _____

    Hint: Look at sentence 1.

Answers

1 Ⓐ Ⓑ Ⓒ Ⓓ   2 Ⓕ Ⓖ Ⓗ Ⓙ

Objective 2: Identifying Supporting Ideas

Sometimes it is helpful to arrange events in the order they happened. This may help you to understand a passage better.

When Gregor Mendel was teaching high school students, he noticed that plants had different traits. For example, some pea plants were tall, while others were short. Mendel wondered why, so he decided to experiment.

Mendel collected the pollen from tall pea plants and put it on the stigmas of the flowers of the short pea plants. He gathered the seeds that were produced. He planted these new seeds and waited for the results. He wondered whether the new plants would be of medium height. Maybe the two traits would blend together. But all the plants that grew from the seeds were tall.

Mendel wanted to see what would happen to the next generation. He crossed the tall plants with each other in the same way he had experimented with the tall and short plants. When the new plants grew, three fourths of the plants were tall, and one fourth were short.

Mendel decided that a plant receives a message from each of its parents, and that message is carried by the plant's genes. For example, a pea plant gets a gene for tallness or shortness from one or both of its parents. Mendel also decided that some genes were stronger than others. The gene for tallness was stronger than the gene for shortness. So a plant would be tall if it had one gene for tallness and one gene for shortness. But if a plant had two genes for shortness, it would be short.

Mendel had made a great discovery, but few understood it at that time. Mendel became famous only after his death.

4 What happened first?

   A Mendel noticed that plants had different traits.

   B Mendel collected pollen from pea plants.

   C Mendel crossed tall plants with each other.

   D Mendel became famous.

Hint: Read the beginning to find out what happened first.

5 Why did Mendel experiment with plants?

   _____
   _____
   _____
   _____

Hint: Look at the first paragraph.

Answers
4 Ⓐ Ⓑ Ⓒ Ⓓ

6 **When did Mendel discover genes?**

    F after he crossed the tall plants with each other

    G while he was working in the garden

    H before he taught high school students

    J before he collected the pollen from tall plants

Hint: Find the section where genes are first mentioned. See what comes before and after that discovery.

7 **When did Mendel become famous?**

    A after his death

    B when he made his great discovery

    C before he became a teacher

    D when he discovered genes

Hint: Look at the last paragraph.

8 **What was one thing Mendel discovered as a result of his experiments?**

_____
_____
_____
_____

Hint: Look at the second and third paragraphs.

Answers

6 F G H J   **7** A B C D

Objective 2: Identifying Supporting Ideas

Written directions tell the reader how to do something. To follow them means to do them in the same order in which they are given.

Peter and his brother opened the box and began to construct the bookcase. They made sure all the parts were in the box by matching them up with the list of parts that also came in the box. The assembly involved different sizes and wooden pegs, screws, and washers; so they laid them out on the floor to make sure they used the right ones in each step. They attached the two sides of the bookcase to the base with the longest screws. The top required the wooden pegs so that they did not show through the surface. The shelf holders were metal, and they inserted them in the predrilled holes in each side of the bookcase. Then it was easy to slide the shelf in. The bookcase was complete.

9 In this paragraph, before the brothers attached the two sides, they —

    F used the wooden pegs.

    G inserted the metal shelf holders.

    H slid the shelf in.

    J laid the pegs and screws on the floor.

Hint: Read the sentence before the one describing how the sides were attached.

Richard was excited about the young tree he had just purchased at the nursery. He was told by the nursery salesperson that he should dig a hole larger than the root system. Then the hole should be watered. Fertilizer and peat moss should be mixed with the soil in the hole before the burlap is cut away from the roots of the tree. After placing the tree in the center of the hole, soil should be added to the hole in such a way that the tree remains upright. Richard should be careful not to allow too much of the tree trunk to be covered with soil. After planting the tree, Richard should water it thoroughly.

10 Along with the tree, Richard needs to buy —

    A a root system.

    B burlap.

    C fertilizer and peat moss.

    D a nursery.

Hint: Make a list of the supplies mentioned in the passage.

11 What is the last thing Richard should do?

_____

_____

_____

_____

Hint: Read the last sentence.

Answers
9 F G H J   10 A B C D

Objective 2: Identifying Supporting Ideas

The setting of a story lets the reader know when and where it is taking place.

In 1848, Joshua Norton went to San Francisco with money in his pocket. Gold had been discovered in California. Many people were making money. Joshua Norton was one of them.

At first, Norton was careful with his money. By 1853, he had saved more than $250,000. But then he invested in rice. Soon after, the price of rice went down. Norton was left without a penny. He vanished for six years.

12 Joshua Norton had saved $250,000 by the year —

F 1853.

G 1953.

H 1848.

J 1859.

Hint: Read sentence 6.

13 Where does the story take place?

_____

_____

_____

Hint: What does the first sentence state?

The art of making perfumes was important in the East. That was where English and French soldiers found the sweet scents in the 1200s. They returned to England and France with the perfumes. Some soldiers even wore perfume into war. They thought it brought them good luck. In the 1500s, perfume was very popular in Europe. In France, Queen Catherine de Medici told her chemist to produce a fragrance for each flower in France. This was the start of a big business there. Even Napoleon had a perfumer. In the next centuries, many famous perfume companies were established.

14 When did the perfume industry begin in France?

A at the time Catherine de Medici was queen

B before the soldiers used it

C at the same time that it was important in the East

D in the next century

Hint: Read the entire passage to determine when the industry began.

15 According to the passage, perfumes were popular in Europe in —

F the 1200s.

G the 1500s.

H the 1700s.

J the 1900s.

Hint: This fact is in the paragraph.

Answers
12 F G H J   14 A B C D   15 F G H J

Objective 3: Summarizing Main Ideas

The main idea is the overall meaning of a piece of writing. Often the main idea is written in the passage.

Bamboo is a giant grass. It grows very fast. One type of bamboo grows three feet in 24 hours! The bamboo is hollow and light but very strong. Bamboo is so strong that it can be made into fences, roofs, boats, and furniture. However, young bamboo is tender, and people eat its beautiful, green shoots.

1. The passage mainly tells that —

   A bamboo can grow quickly.

   B bamboo looks like giant grass.

   C people eat bamboo plants.

   D the bamboo plant is very useful.

   Hint: What does the whole story talk about?

People once played football bareheaded. After many injuries, players began to wear plain leather caps. Plastic helmets and masks appeared later. Still, many players were getting hurt. To make the helmets better, designers studied woodpeckers! Their tough, spongy skulls became the model for modern football helmets.

2. What is the main idea of the story?

   F Football helmets must be strong and light.

   G Leather caps were used in football at one time.

   H The woodpecker had a role in football helmet design.

   J Many football players are injured.

   Hint: What point does the story make?

Rescuers fought to free a man caught in a burning truck. The metal was so badly twisted that even a wrecker couldn't budge it. Then, suddenly a stranger ripped a door off the cab with his bare hands, twisted the steering wheel away, and braced his shoulders under the crushed top to lift it. Later, people found out that the stranger had once lost a child in a fire. His hatred of fire apparently gave him the enormous strength to save the trapped man.

3. What is the main idea of this story?

   A A man got caught in a fire.

   B A trapped man needed to be freed from a wrecked truck.

   C The stranger was very strong.

   D A man's emotions helped him save a life.

   Hint: What is the point of the story?

North Carolina police may use germs to catch bank thieves. Important papers can be sprayed with harmless germs that will stick to the hands of anyone who touches the papers. If a dishonest employee steals the papers, anything that he or she touches will have the germs on it. A scientist can show that the person leaving the germs got them when stealing the treated papers.

4. What is this passage mainly about?

   _____
   _____
   _____
   _____

   Hint: What does the whole story talk about?

Answers

1 Ⓐ Ⓑ Ⓒ Ⓓ   2 Ⓕ Ⓖ Ⓗ Ⓙ   3 Ⓐ Ⓑ Ⓒ Ⓓ

Objective 3: Summarizing Main Ideas

Often the main idea is not given in the text. Sometimes the reader needs to draw his or her own conclusion by putting the facts together.

As a child, Jane Goodall loved to study animals and insects. She took notes on birds and bugs. She even opened a small museum for her friends. She hoped to travel to Africa when she grew up. At age 23, she got her wish and went to Kenya. She stayed in Africa and has become a famous scientist. Her field of study is the behavior of chimpanzees. Goodall has claimed her success is due to patience, courage, observation, and willpower.

5   What is the implied main idea of this selection?

   F   If you don't start a field of study as a child, you will never be a success.

   G   Jane Goodall went to Africa at the age of 23.

   H   Patience and courage will develop a person's love of animals.

   J   Jane Goodall developed her childhood love of animals and insects into a career as a famous scientist.

Hint: Read the entire passage to determine the implied main idea.

Allison was upset over a difficult homework problem. She had been working on it for a while, but she still couldn't get the answer. "Why don't we go outside for a walk?" her dad suggested. Allison looked up at the stars as they walked. Her dad pointed out the planet Venus. When they returned home, Allison felt ready to tackle the homework problem. "Thanks for the walk, Dad," she said.

6   What is the main idea of this selection?

   _____
   _____
   _____
   _____

Hint: Read the entire paragraph to determine the implied main idea.

Jessica had often seen people sleeping on the sidewalks downtown. Usually, she didn't think twice about them. But one day, she saw a young mother with two small children. They were getting food from a trash can behind a cafe. The sight made Jessica cry, and she promised herself she would do something to help. The next day, she began a food drive for the homeless.

7   What is the main idea implied in this selection?

   A   Jessica felt sorry for homeless people.

   B   The homeless people slept on sidewalks.

   C   A mother got food from a trash can.

   D   Jessica realized that the homeless need help.

Hint: Read the entire passage to determine the implied main idea.

Answers
5   Ⓕ Ⓖ Ⓗ Ⓙ   7   Ⓐ Ⓑ Ⓒ Ⓓ

Objective 3: Summarizing Main Ideas

A good summary contains the main idea of a passage. It is brief, yet it covers the most important points.

The Masai of East Africa raise cattle for a living. Very little grain is raised in the area, so the people depend on the cattle for food. Most people drink a gallon of milk a day, and beef is a popular meat. Cow's blood is also used as food. It doesn't spoil, it provides protein and minerals, and it can be taken from cows while traveling.

8 What is this passage mostly about?

    F There is much grain raised in the world.

    G People in different areas of the world eat odd foods.

    H Cows provide food for the Masai.

    J There are many different kinds of cattle raised by the Masai.

Hint: Which choice tells you about the whole passage?

Plant experts in Bolivia have found some odd potato plants. The potato leaves make a sticky glue. Insects that walk on the plant get caught and starve. Scientists want to breed more potatoes with these sticky leaves. Farmers would be able to grow potatoes and not have to spray their plants with chemicals to get rid of insects.

9 What is this passage mostly about?

    A Insects are caught by potato plants.

    B Potato plants grow in Bolivia.

    C A special potato plant may be helpful to farmers.

    D Chemical sprays help to kill insects.

Hint: Which choice tells you about the whole passage?

In colonial times, women were printers, whalers, and blacksmiths. Today, women are fighting hard to get some of these jobs. For years, men didn't deliver babies, but now there are many male doctors. Women's work used to be sewing, cooking, and raising children. But in 1960, the first female prime minister in the world was elected.

10 How have jobs changed over time?

_____

_____

_____

_____

Hint: Read the entire paragraph to find the answer.

Answers
8 F G H J   9 A B C D

One hundred viruses placed side by side would be no wider than a human hair. But these germs cause more than fifty diseases. Chicken pox, colds, and rabies are all caused by viruses. More than 21 million people have died from the flu caused by these germs. Scientists are seeking ways to get rid of these tiny killers.

11 **What is this passage mostly about?**

    F Tiny viruses cause deadly diseases.

    G Many people die from the flu.

    H Chicken pox is caused by a virus.

    J Many people have died from viruses.

Hint: Which sentence tells you about the whole passage?

The rare Chinese panda lives on tender, young bamboo shoots. But most bamboo plants die right after flowering. Without the bamboo, the pandas starve. Because some people fear that the rare pandas may die out, in some places food is given to the hungry animals. Some pandas are airlifted to places where bamboo is still plentiful.

12 **What is the best summary of this passage?**

    A Chinese pandas usually eat bamboo.

    B The flower of the bamboo plant is beautiful, but deadly.

    C People are working to keep rare pandas alive.

    D Pandas die without enough young bamboo shoots to eat.

Hint: Pick the choice that best covers the main point of the passage.

The spots on a fawn's coat let it hide in shady areas without being seen. The viceroy butterfly looks like the bad-tasting monarch, so birds avoid both. The hognose snake hisses and rolls on its back when it fears another animal. When the opossum is attacked, it plays dead. Distressed turtles hide in their shells until they're sure it's safe to come out again.

13 **What is the main idea of this story?**

    _____

    _____

    _____

    _____

Hint: All of the sentences together give you the main idea of this paragraph.

Answers
11 Ⓕ Ⓖ Ⓗ Ⓙ   12 Ⓐ Ⓑ Ⓒ Ⓓ

Objective 4: Perceiving Relationships and Recognizing Outcomes

Often when we read, we need to see cause-and-effect relationships. Knowing what caused a given event or a character's actions will help us to better understand what we read.

In the years before the American Civil War, there was a federal law that allowed slave owners to reclaim their escaped slaves. Anthony Burns was born a slave in Virginia. He escaped to Boston in 1854. He lived and worked there for a few months before his former owner appeared and had him arrested. The trial of Anthony Burns triggered angry mobs in Boston, a city where most people were against slavery. He was forced to go back to Virginia with his master, but he later gained his freedom.

1 Why was Anthony Burns arrested?

A He was born a slave.

B The angry mobs in Boston were against him.

C His owner was allowed by law to reclaim him.

D He was living and working in Boston.

Hint: Being arrested is the effect. What caused this to happen?

Joan was attending a concert with her parents. After the first few minutes, she noticed an odd smell. She whispered to her parents about it. Her parents realized that there was a gas leak in the building. They calmly alerted the ushers. Joan noticed a woman starting to faint as one of the ushers stepped up to the microphone to make an announcement.

2 What made Joan whisper?

F She noticed an odd smell.

G She didn't like the concert after the first few minutes.

H She thought the usher was cute.

J She noticed a woman starting to faint.

Hint: Whispering is the effect. What made this happen?

Matt was playing ball in the backyard when his sister burst from the house. "Chris has a piece of candy stuck in her throat and can't breathe!" she shouted. Matt quickly ran inside and found Chris lying on the floor. She was turning blue. Remembering some of his first-aid training, Matt picked up Chris and wrapped his arms just below her chest. He pushed in and up three times. Suddenly, Chris started to cry.

3 Why did Chris start to cry?

_____

_____

_____

_____

Hint: Making Chris cry is the effect. What made this happen?

Answers

1 Ⓐ Ⓑ Ⓒ Ⓓ   **2** Ⓕ Ⓖ Ⓗ Ⓙ

Objective 4: Perceiving Relationships and Recognizing Outcomes

Often the reader can predict, or tell in advance, what is probably going to happen next. The reader must think about what would make sense if the story were to continue.

"I'll race you to my house!" Meg shouted. Jane struggled to catch up with her. She ran through the deep snow. Both girls dragged their sleds behind them. As soon as they reached the house, they pulled off their wet mittens, scarves, caps, boots, and coats. Meg made hot chocolate and offered some to Jane.

4 What might happen next?

- **A** Jane and Meg will drink hot chocolate.
- **B** The girls will clean Meg's room.
- **C** The girls will clean their clothes.
- **D** Jane will go back outside to play.

Hint: Which of the choices would most likely come next?

Pat couldn't get the awful conversation out of her mind. She had been so angry with Kate that she had said some things she didn't really mean. Now she wished she had put a big piece of tape over her mouth. Then she noticed the telephone on the kitchen wall. She grabbed the receiver and started to dial.

5 What will Pat probably do next?

- **F** call Kate and apologize
- **G** call to order take-out food
- **H** call her mother to ask her what she should do
- **J** call for the weather report

Hint: Think about how Pat feels.

Hope and Dave were playing a game of checkers. Their parents were out for the evening. The wind had been howling for several minutes. They heard the tornado siren go off. But before they could scramble down the basement stairs, the lights went out. The next thing Dave knew, his sister was screaming. In the dim light, Dave saw that a beam had fallen from the ceiling and trapped Hope.

6 What will probably happen next?

_____
_____
_____
_____

Hint: What would you most likely do next if you were Dave?

Answers
4 Ⓐ Ⓑ Ⓒ Ⓓ   5 Ⓕ Ⓖ Ⓗ Ⓙ

Objective 5: Making Inferences and Generalizations

Sometimes a passage will have a graph or diagram with it. These are there to help the reader better understand the passage.

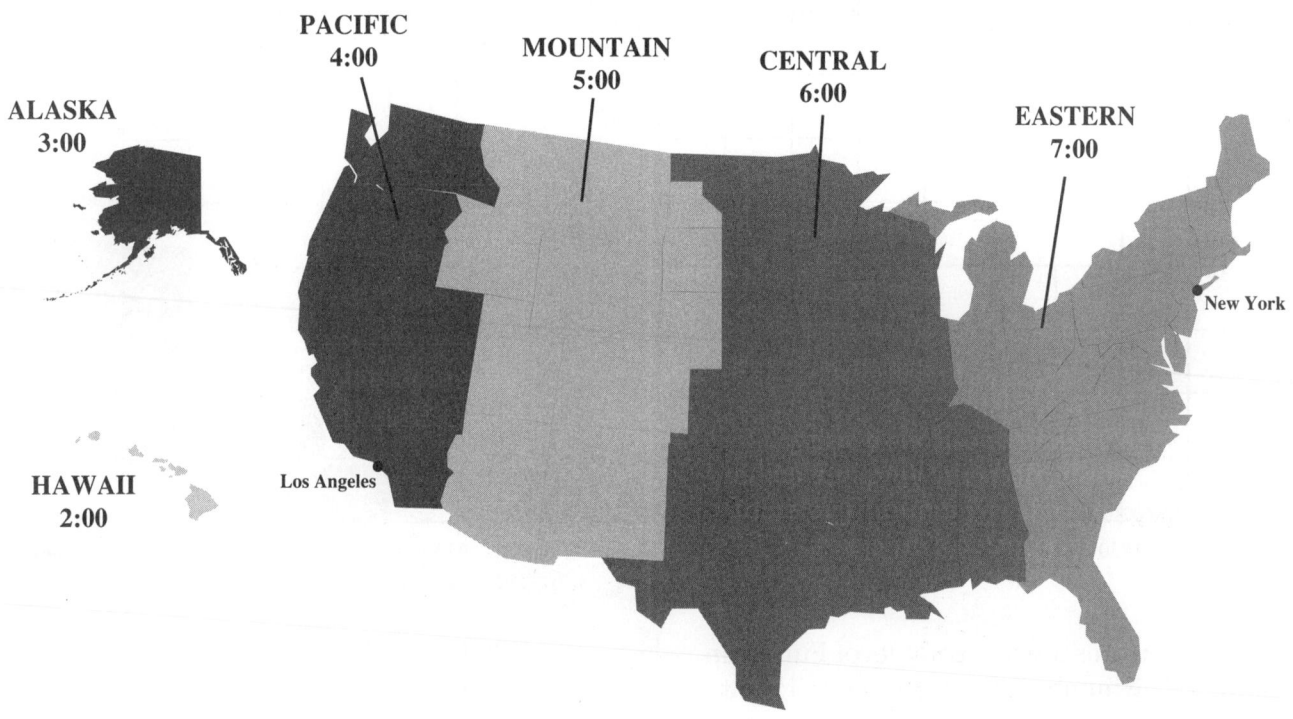

The United States is divided into six time zones. People on the West Coast are three hours behind people on the East Coast. Hawaiians are five hours behind Floridians. Rhode Islanders are four hours ahead of Alaskans.

1. If Tanya in New York wanted to call her friend in Los Angeles at noon Los Angeles time, at what time would Tanya have to make the call?

    A 9:00 A.M.

    B noon

    C 3:00 P.M.

    D 9:00 P.M.

    Hint: Look at New York and Los Angeles on the map to see which time zones they are in.

Answers
1 Ⓐ Ⓑ Ⓒ Ⓓ

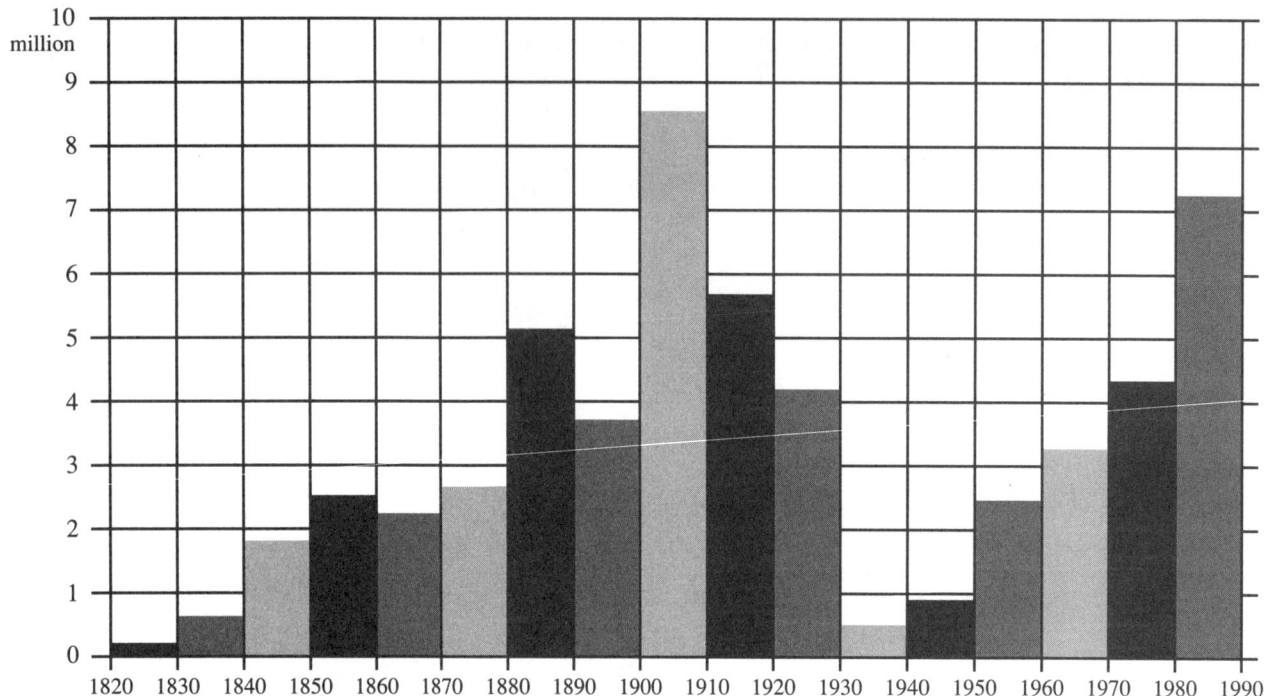

Many Americans are descendants of European immigrants. The number of European immigrants to the United States grew until a national quota system was set in 1921. The quota system was abolished in 1965. During the 1970s, 1.6 million people came from Asia alone to settle in the United States. Immigration today is more carefully controlled, and only about half a million people a year are allowed to settle in the United States.

2 What is the largest amount of immigrants to come to the United States in a decade between 1820 and 1990?

F about 7.5 million

G 10 million

H almost 9 million

J 6 million

Hint: Read the graph to find out the number of immigrants each decade.

Answers

2 Ⓕ Ⓖ Ⓗ Ⓙ

Objective 5: Making Inferences and Generalizations

A logical conclusion is an ending that makes sense. Often it can be proved true by the information given in the paragraph.

Women, in general, have shorter vocal cords than men. Shorter cords vibrate faster, which makes the pitch of the voice higher. This causes women to have higher voices. Women also need less air to vibrate their vocal cords. That allows women to be able to talk longer and with less effort than men.

3 You can conclude that women —

  A talk louder than men.

  B have vocal cords that vibrate faster than men's.

  C talk faster than men.

  D talk more than men.

Hint: Pick the choice that can be proved true by what's in the passage.

Many people take aspirin for aches and pains. Aspirin was first sold around 1900 by the Bayer Company of Germany. It was sold under the trademark "Aspirin." Then World War I swept across the world, and Germany lost the war. Under its terms of surrender, Germany agreed to release the trademark. The name "Aspirin" could no longer be used to sell only Bayer's product. It became the common name of a drug for pain.

4 From the passage you can tell that —

  F Germany did not fight in World War I.

  G aspirin was first sold in Greenland.

  H an unusual term of surrender was met.

  J aspirin is no longer sold anywhere.

Hint: You must read the entire paragraph, especially the last three sentences.

Some people believe in the luck that charms can bring. This was the case of Mary Hopf. She was to compete in a race for the Junior Olympics in Nebraska. When Hopf discovered that she had forgotten her charms at home in Pennsylvania, she panicked. Suddenly, she remembered that her race would be shown on television. Hopf made a long-distance call to her sister. Her sister placed the charms on top of the television set. Hopf won the race.

5 Why did Mary win the race?

_____
_____
_____
_____

Hint: Think about what it takes for someone to win a race.

Answers
3 Ⓐ Ⓑ Ⓒ Ⓓ   4 Ⓕ Ⓖ Ⓗ Ⓙ

Objective 5: Making Inferences and Generalizations

Sometimes a reader needs to generalize. This means to come up with a general statement about something in the text.

Working at home sounds like fun. You can work in your pajamas. Or you can play the radio as loud as you want. You can even sleep an extra hour in the morning. But making money at home takes drive and dedication. To be successful you must use basic business practices. You must make yourself work rather than play.

6 You can tell from the paragraph that to be successful you probably need to —

   A stock the refrigerator with plenty of food.

   B make a schedule and stick to it.

   C plan when to take naps.

   D work as little as possible.

Hint: Read the last two sentences in the paragraph.

The Egyptian pyramids were built from stones weighing about two and one-half tons each. The structures are forty stories high. The number of stones used in each pyramid could build a wall around France. Yet the Egyptians used no animals. They had no cranes at that time. The wheel wasn't even in use.

7 From this paragraph, you can make the generalization that —

   F the Egyptians built a wall around France.

   G the pyramids must have been built by many people.

   H the pyramids were two and one-half stories high.

   J each pyramid weighed about two and one-half tons.

Hint: Eliminate the choices that can be proved untrue.

When the Tacoma Narrows Bridge was built in 1940, it was the third largest suspension bridge in the world. Large suspension bridges had been built before. But the builders didn't count on the winds near Tacoma, Washington. Four months after its opening, the bridge was blown down.

8 Why didn't other earlier bridges have problems?

   _____
   _____
   _____
   _____

Hint: Why did the Tacoma Narrows Bridge collapse?

Answers
6 Ⓐ Ⓑ Ⓒ Ⓓ   7 Ⓕ Ⓖ Ⓗ Ⓙ

Objective 5: Making Inferences and Generalizations

A good reader will sum up what he or she reads and make his or her own judgment about the text. Often things are implied in a text, rather than stated directly.

Sleepwalking is most common among children 10 to 12 years of age. Experts think that it is linked to the growth and development of children. Most sleepwalkers just sit up in bed or stand near their bed. Some people, however, may walk around. Those who walk around can easily hurt themselves. It does not harm sleepwalkers to awaken them, but they may be so confused that they will strike out. After awakening, sleepwalkers don't remember what they did.

9 After reading the passage, you can assume that —

A sleepwalkers can be violent.

B sleepwalkers are really awake.

C sleepwalkers are aware of what they're doing.

D sleepwalkers are not aware of what they're doing.

Hint: Read each of the choices carefully. Which one makes the most sense?

In an interview, world-renowned scientist Albert Einstein was once asked whether he got his great thoughts while in the bathtub, walking, or sitting in his office. Einstein replied, "I don't really know. I've only had one or maybe two."

10 From this story you might think that Einstein —

F was a modest man.

G did not think his ideas were good.

H took a lot of baths.

J did not really know much.

Hint: Read the entire paragraph.

Harvey Gartley of Michigan did not really want to become a boxer. Maybe that's why he lost a fight without ever being hit. The boy was in a Golden Gloves match. As his opponent swung and jabbed, Gartley danced just out of reach. But he danced too much and soon fell down from exhaustion. The match was over in 47 seconds. When Gartley lost, his parents were disappointed.

11 What can you conclude about Gartley's parents?

_____

_____

_____

_____

Hint: You need to read the entire paragraph and put together the facts before drawing a conclusion.

Answers
9 Ⓐ Ⓑ Ⓒ Ⓓ   10 Ⓕ Ⓖ Ⓗ Ⓙ

Objective 5: Making Inferences and Generalizations

The way a person in a story acts tells the reader about how the character feels. Other clues may be what is said to or about the character.

Once a poor student had to wander about the countryside. He had no money, and he had no home. One freezing night, the student knocked at the door of a farmer's house. The farmer was an agreeable person who said, "Come in! You look very tired and hungry." The farmer gave the student supper, and the two began talking. The farmer asked whether the student could answer a question he was wondering about. He asked, "What is it that the gods are doing up in the sky tonight?" The student pondered for a long time but confessed that he didn't know the answer. "Never mind," said the farmer. "Maybe there is no answer."

The farmer gave the student a cozy room in which to sleep and a big breakfast the next morning. "Now," said the student, "I'll be on my way. Thank you."

The student traveled on. He eventually found a good job as a teacher and purchased a home of his own. One day, the teacher saw a very old fellow limping up the path. His hair was white, and his clothes were ragged. The teacher invited the old man in. He fed the man, and they talked. The younger man recognized the stranger as the farmer who assisted him long ago.

The teacher said, "Now I know the answer to the question you asked me. The gods were constructing a wheel that turns very slowly. Someday the person at the top will be at the bottom, and the person at the bottom will be at the top. And since we are all on the same wheel, my friend, you may live in my house in comfort all the days of your life."

12 How did the farmer feel when the student knocked on his door?

  A angry because he had to give him supper

  B angry because the student could not answer his question

  C pleased that he was able to help the student

  D scared

Hint: Read the section to which the question refers.

13 How did the teacher feel after he recognized the stranger?

  F angry that the old man had tricked him

  G happy that he had learned a very important lesson in life

  H determined to invest in Ferris wheels

  J sure that the farmer would be a great handy man

Hint: Read the last four sentences.

14 How was the student feeling when he knocked at the farmer's door?

  _____
  _____
  _____
  _____

Hint: Read the first three sentences to determine how the student felt.

Answers
12 Ⓐ Ⓑ Ⓒ Ⓓ   13 Ⓕ Ⓖ Ⓗ Ⓙ

Objective 6: Recognizing Points of View, Facts, and Opinions

The author's point of view is what he or she thinks or feels about what he or she is writing. Opinions express points of view.

Ali Baba was a poor, hard-working man. He supported himself and his family by selling wood. He often journeyed high up into the mountains to cut down trees. By himself, he would load the wood he had cut onto his donkeys. Then he would take it into the village where he lived and sell it. He didn't make much money, but it was all he could do.

One day, after he had just finished cutting a load of wood, Ali Baba saw many men on their horses. The men were wearing armor and carrying weapons. Their horses were loaded with huge sacks. Ali Baba knew that the men were thieves. He was afraid that they would kill him, so he climbed up into a tree to hide from them. Ali Baba watched silently from his hiding place as forty thieves approached a huge rock. "Open, Sesame!" called their leader. A small door opened, and the thieves carried their stolen gold into the cave. After the thieves left, Ali Baba hastened to the rock and called, "Open, Sesame!" When the cave door opened, Ali Baba went inside, seized the gold, and took it home with him. He had a new home built for his family. He gave them the things they deserved.

Soon, the thieves found that their treasure was gone. They were furious. They rode into the village where Ali Baba lived. The leader asked villagers if anyone had recently become rich. A man mentioned Ali Baba. The leader of the thieves hid his men inside enormous oil jars. He asked if he might leave the jars at Ali Baba's house until it was time to go to market the next morning. Ali Baba welcomed the man, offering to help him out. He did not recognize him as the leader of the thieves. The thieves planned to sneak out of the jars during the night, take back the gold, and kill Ali Baba and his family. But Ali Baba's servant grew curious. She inspected the jars, saw the sleeping thieves, and tied them all up.

1. You can tell that the author thinks —

   A Ali Baba did not take good care of his family.

   B Ali Baba was a lazy man.

   C Ali Baba should not have taken all the gold.

   D Ali Baba deserves his good fortune.

   Hint: Think about how Ali Baba is described throughout the passage.

2. How would the author probably describe Ali Baba's servant?

   _____
   _____
   _____
   _____

   Hint: How does the author feel about the thieves? Does the author think they got the fate they deserved?

Answers
1 Ⓐ Ⓑ Ⓒ Ⓓ

Objective 6: Recognizing Points of View, Facts, and Opinions

When an author wants to convince the reader of something, her or she uses language that backs up his or her point of view. Often the language is very descriptive and emotional.

The word "natural" appears in large letters across many cans and boxes of food. But this word, and others like it, sometimes give shoppers false ideas about the food inside. Even though laws require that all food labels give truthful information, this does not always happen.

The word "natural" has not been defined by the FDA, the agency in charge of food labels. So any food maker can use the word on a package. Even the worst junk food is certain to have something natural in it. So the makers of these foods can use "natural" on their packages.

Consumers should read labels carefully and write letters of complaint to the FDA whenever they come across products that are not truly natural. Everyone in the marketplace can help to make truth in labeling work effectively.

3   What is the author trying to persuade the reader to do?

   F   help monitor the truth-in-labeling laws

   G   write betters labels for consumer goods

   H   eat junk food because it is natural in part

   J   go shopping more often

Hint: Read the first and last paragraphs.

4   The author states, "Even the worst junk food is certain to have something natural in it." What is the author trying to convince the reader of?

   _____
   _____
   _____
   _____

Hint: Reread the sentence and the sentences before and after it.

Answers
3 Ⓕ Ⓖ Ⓗ Ⓙ

Objective 6: Recognizing Points of View, Facts and Opinions

It is important to recognize the difference between fact and opinion. A fact is real and true. An opinion states a point of view. Words that describe are used to offer opinions.

A dozen small turtles slide off a rock and slip into a pond. These turtles look as if an artist had painted them. Pale-yellow stripes cross their upper shells, and a red border circles the edge. More red and yellow stripes are on the turtles' heads, and just behind each eye is another yellow spot.

These eastern painted turtles live in marshy areas, ponds, and slow-moving rivers. They like to be in places where rocks and fallen trees project from the water. The turtles like to climb out onto the rocks or dead trees to sleep in the warm sunlight. If something frightens them, they slide quickly into the water.

5 Which of the following is an opinion?

  A Painted turtles are prettier than other kinds.

  B Eastern painted turtles live in marshy ponds.

  C The turtles like to sleep in the warm sunlight.

  D Turtles go back into the water when something frightens them.

Hint: A fact is real and true. Look for words that are opinions.

Giant sequoia trees grow near the coast of northern California. Sequoia trees are also called redwoods. For many years, experts thought that these tall trees were the oldest living trees on earth. In 1892, one of the trees was cut down. Scientists counted the growth rings in the tree to find out its age. They discovered that the tree was indeed old. It had lived for about 3,212 years. Today, experts know that the redwood trees average about 3,500 years in age.

Redwoods have straight trunks and branches that seem to brush against the sky. One redwood, named "General Sherman," is the largest living thing in the world. It is 272 feet tall.

In 1953, scientists became interested in another type of tree. They had discovered some very old bristlecone pines in Nevada. At heights of only twenty to sixty feet, these pines were not as grand as the redwoods. But the experts began to wonder if they were older.

In 1957, they found a pine over 4,000 years old. Their theory had been correct. Further study turned up even older trees. One of these trees, "Methuselah," is the oldest living tree in the world. It is 4,700 years old. But even though some pine trees may be older, most do not live as long as the redwoods. This is because the redwoods have a longer life span.

6 Which of the following is an opinion?

  F Pine trees don't look as nice as giant sequoias.

  G Pine trees are older than sequoias.

  H The largest living redwood is 272 feet tall.

  J Old bristlecone pines were discovered in Nevada.

Hint: Look for words that express a feeling, not a fact.

7 Which of the following is an opinion from the passage?

  A Redwoods are also called sequoias.

  B To find out the age of a tree, scientists count its rings.

  C The straight trunk and branches of the redwood make it the most magnificent tree.

  D The average age of a redwood tree is 3,500 years.

Hint: What is actually said in the passage? Which sentence is not always true?

"What an ugly boy!" many people whispered when they saw Hans Christian Andersen. His hands and feet were gigantic. His eyes were tiny, and his nose was too big for such a thin face. He seemed clumsy as he clattered to school in his wooden shoes. Young Hans lived a sad life. His father was a poor shoemaker, and his mother was often ill. So the lonely boy created a make-believe world of this own, designing toy theaters and carving tiny figures to act in them.

In 1819, when Hans was 14, he made a big decision. He left his home and traveled across Denmark to the city of Copenhagen. "Here," declared Hans, "I will make my dream come true. I will become a famous actor." But it soon became evident that the dream would not come true at all. For three years, Hans tried to find an acting job but had no luck. When he was 17, Hans sadly returned home.

Hans went back to school and worked hard at his lessons. He kept a journal, which he filled with his dreams, thoughts, and ideas for stories. In his journal, Hans told about an ugly bird that was laughed at by the ducklings in the farmyard. But the little bird was not a duck at all, and it grew into an elegant swan.

Hans graduated from school with a new dream of becoming a famous writer of novels and articles. He kept busy at his writing. But publishers would not buy his books or his news stories, and it seemed that this dream, too, would never come true. By the time he was thirty, Hans was very poor indeed. He decided to try writing stories for children. Adults and children loved these stories! People of all ages do. Andersen's best story is "The Ugly Duckling." In a way it is the story of Andersen himself.

8 **Which of the following is an opinion?**

F Hans tried to be an actor.

G Hans did not have a very happy childhood.

H Hans dreamed of becoming a famous writer.

J Han's best story is "The Ugly Duckling."

Hint: An opinion is someone's point of view, and not a fact.

9 **Write two facts you learned about Hans Christian Andersen from reading this story.**

_____

_____

_____

_____

Hint: A fact is something real and true. An opinion is what you think of something.

Answers
8 Ⓕ Ⓖ Ⓗ Ⓙ

UNIT THREE
Reading Comprehension

Directions: Read the selection carefully. Then read each question. Darken the circle for the correct answer, or write the answer in the space provided.

TRY THIS — More than one answer choice may sound correct. Choose the answer that goes best with the story.

Sample A Sylvia's First Day

Sylvia's first day of school was difficult. She had just moved from another state. Sylvia felt lonely and scared as she tried to find her classrooms. Nothing seemed to go right that day at school.

Which word best describes Sylvia's feelings about the first day at her new school?

A unhappy
B joyful
C confident
D angry

THINK IT THROUGH — The correct answer is A. This was Sylvia's first day at a new school. The third sentence states that Sylvia was lonely and scared. The word unhappy best describes those feelings.

My Favorite Sport

Racing, Sweating
Bouncing, Jamming
Passing, Catching
Shooting, Dunking
Swishing, Jumping

All these actions make my body sore.
But I love to hear the crowd roar.
The noise lifts me out of my seat.
My ears hurt, though, when there's a defeat,
From the silence that bounces off the walls.
I go home reviewing the ref's calls.
I look forward to the next game.
They are always different, never the same.

1 Which of the following best describes the tone of the poem?

A jealousy
B sadness
C liveliness
D boredom

2 According to the poem, what makes the poet's ears hurt?

F the roar of the crowd
G the noise from bouncing
H the jumping out of the seat
J the silence that bounces off the walls

3 What sport does this poem describe?

_____
_____
_____
_____

Answers
SA Ⓐ Ⓑ Ⓒ Ⓓ   1 Ⓐ Ⓑ Ⓒ Ⓓ   2 Ⓕ Ⓖ Ⓗ Ⓙ

Outdoor Adventure

For weeks Jeff had been looking forward to the trip. He and his father were going snow camping in Yellowstone National Park. The two had been running several miles a day for *stamina*. They knew it wouldn't be easy to cross-country ski into the wilderness carrying heavy backpacks. They prepared for the trip by reading books about winter camping, and they carefully planned which gear they would take for the trip.

Finally the big day arrived. Jeff and his father rose early and drove to the entrance to the park. Mr. Cawley talked to the park rangers. He showed them the route they planned to take and where they would camp each night. The rangers said the weather and snow conditions were good for skiing and wished them a good trip. Jeff and his father strapped on their back packs and skied away from the car.

Jeff felt a little nervous at first. It was strange to be leaving the city behind and entering such a cold, empty land. The rangers said that Jeff and his father probably would not see anyone else on their excursion, although there was a chance they would see coyotes or bears. As Jeff's legs warmed up and he got into the rhythm of skiing, he felt less fearful. Rolling white hills stretched as far as he could see. The fir trees were dusted with snow, and a peaceful silence surrounded the two skiers. Jeff began to feel as if he were entering an enchanted land.

After a few hours, Jeff and his father rounded a bend and saw an elk standing a short distance away. Its head was down, and it made no effort to run. They stopped and watched it. "Something's wrong with it," Mr. Cawley commented. "It's probably old or sick. Maybe it's starving."

"It won't last long out here," Jeff said, remembering the coyotes and bears the rangers had told them about.

"You're right about that," his father replied.

A few miles later, the skiers entered a canyon formed by the Madison River. This was where they had decided to make their first campsite. "It feels great to take off this heavy pack," Jeff thought. Both he and his father had brought lightweight shovels. They began digging a pit in the snow. They chose a place in the open, away from the trees, where the morning sun would warm them. They used ski poles as center supports and slung the tarp over the pit. Then they piled snow on the edges of the tarp to form a snug, wind-proof shelter.

Jeff unpacked a cooking pot and walked to the river to get water. He watched huge trout swim by in the clear, icy river. Maybe he could catch some trout for breakfast, but just then he was too tired and hungry to think about fishing. He wanted something hot to drink and a quick, easy dinner. Jeff and his father crawled into their shelter and lit the camp stove. The freeze-dried dinners were simple to prepare. They simply had to pour boiling water into the pouches and stir the contents.

The temperature dropped quickly as soon as the sun set, so Jeff and his father decided to go to bed early. A few hours later, they were awakened by a loud, eerie baying. Coyotes! Jeff felt as if his heart froze. It sounded as if hundreds of coyotes were right outside the tarp. What would they do if they were surrounded by hungry coyotes?

Mr. Cawley lifted the tarp and looked out. "I can't see anything. I think they're up the canyon a mile or two," he said. "The howling is echoing off the canyon walls, making them sound nearer than they really are." Jeff and his father exchanged looks. Both of them were thinking about the elk they had passed that afternoon.

The next morning, they got out of their sleeping bags and were glad to see that the day was bright and beautiful. Jeff was surprised when he opened his contact lens case. The liquid they were soaking in had frozen! When he stepped outside, he saw vapor rising from the river like steam. It was so cold they decided not to fish, but to pack up and get moving right away.

"Why don't we leave our packs here, and ski back to where we saw the elk?" Jeff suggested.

Mr. Cawley agreed, and without the packs they skied easily. From a distance they could see that they had guessed right. The elk's skeleton lay in the valley surrounded by numerous coyote tracks. Jeff had read about animals in the wild, but had never before witnessed their struggle for survival. He shivered as he wondered what else they would see in the wilderness.

4 Another good title for this story would be—

A "Building a Wind-Proof Shelter."

B "Falling Through Frozen Ice."

C "Preparing Freeze-Dried Food."

D "Witnessing the Frozen Wilderness."

5 Which words describe Jeff's reaction when he heard the coyotes howling?

F "felt as if his heart froze"

G "felt a little nervous"

H "felt fearless"

J "felt tired and hungry"

6 What time of year did Jeff and his father go camping?

A during the summer

B during late spring

C during the winter

D during the fall

7 In this story, *excursion* means—

F a short journey.

G a vacation.

H a snowmobile.

J a brief map.

8 This story mainly shows that Jeff and his father—

A had been preparing for and looking forward to this trip for weeks.

B were very tired after their first day of skiing.

C went on a ski trip and experienced some of the realities of life in the wilderness.

D camped beside the Madison River and were awakened by coyotes.

9 As Jeff and his father skied away from the car, Jeff can best be described as—

F happy.

G excited.

H anxious.

J tired.

10 If a person has *stamina,* it means that the person has—

A wealth.

B reasoning powers.

C the ability to put up with strain and hardship.

D the power to fast for several days.

11 Mr. Cawley probably showed the rangers the route they planned to take so the rangers—

F could come and keep them company.

G would know where to look for them if they did not return.

H would know where to phone them.

J could keep the wild animals away from them.

12 Why did Mr. Cawley think there was something wrong with the elk?

_____

_____

_____

_____

Answers

4 Ⓐ Ⓑ Ⓒ Ⓓ   6 Ⓐ Ⓑ Ⓒ Ⓓ   8 Ⓐ Ⓑ Ⓒ Ⓓ   10 Ⓐ Ⓑ Ⓒ Ⓓ

5 Ⓕ Ⓖ Ⓗ Ⓙ   7 Ⓕ Ⓖ Ⓗ Ⓙ   9 Ⓕ Ⓖ Ⓗ Ⓙ   11 Ⓕ Ⓖ Ⓗ Ⓙ

Daily Schedule
Fairfield Outdoor Education Center
Leonard Middle School

The following schedule shows a typical day at Fairfield Outdoor Education Center. Seating for meals is always at 8:00 A.M. for breakfast; 11:30 A.M. for lunch; and 5:00 P.M. for dinner. The rest of the program is quite flexible, depending on the needs of individual students, on the availability of teachers, and on the weather conditions.

Time	Activity
6:30–7:30 A.M.	Wake up. Make beds. Clean dorm rooms. Girls shower. Boys run laps around the lake.
7:30–8:00 A.M.	One group of students sets breakfast table. Another group of students prepares day packs for outdoor activities.
8:00–9:00 A.M.	Eat breakfast. Group that sets the table washes the dishes. Other group writes in journals.
9:00–11:30 A.M.	Instructional period. Students learn the proper techniques of hiking, skiing, and canoeing. Students learn about the plants and animals that live in Fairfield. Students use journals, sketch pads, binoculars, and cameras to help them record their sightings.
11:30 A.M.–12:30 P.M.	Lunch, dishwashing, and dorm break.
12:30–4:30 P.M.	Instructional period. Students explore a swamp area, a large granite quarry, and a dry creek bed. Students learn to hunt for fossils. Students use mallets, chiseling tools, journals, clipboards, sketch pads, and cameras to help them find and record ancient fossils.
4:30–5:00 P.M.	Silent reading time.
5:00–6:00 P.M.	Dinner, dishwashing, and dorm break.
6:00–9:00 P.M.	Students play a variety of games, such as volleyball. After dusk a campfire is started. Students identify constellations and nocturnal animals while on a night walk.
9:00–10:00 P.M.	Boys shower. Girls exercise. All students prepare for sleep.
10:00 P.M.	Lights out.
Final Night 6:00–9:00 P.M.	Families of all students are invited to a hot-dog roast. Students perform skits to show what they have learned.

13 If a student's afternoon instructional period doesn't end until 5:00 P.M., the student will miss—

  A dinner.
  B a dorm break.
  C silent reading time.
  D dishwashing.

14 There is enough information in this schedule to show that—

  F students are expected to do very little work in this program.
  G students spend most of their day learning about outdoor activities.
  H students will be at the Fairfield Outdoor Education Center for one week.
  J boys and girls do not attend the education center at the same time.

15 Which activity do the students participate in after lunch?

  A write in journals
  B hunt for fossils
  C canoe on the lake
  D ski through woods

16 What does the group that is not setting the breakfast table do between 7:30 and 8:00 A.M.?

  F prepares day packs
  G makes beds
  H runs laps
  J washes the dishes

17 Who will participate in this outdoor education program?

  A high school students from all over the state
  B middle school students from Leonard
  C middle school students in scout groups
  D high school students from the county who study biology

18 Why will the students perform skits at the Final Night activities?

  _____
  _____
  _____
  _____

Answers
13 Ⓐ Ⓑ Ⓒ Ⓓ   14 Ⓕ Ⓖ Ⓗ Ⓙ   15 Ⓐ Ⓑ Ⓒ Ⓓ   16 Ⓕ Ⓖ Ⓗ Ⓙ   17 Ⓐ Ⓑ Ⓒ Ⓓ

Helen Keller Remembers
by Helen Keller

The morning after my teacher came she led me into her room and gave me a doll. I had played with it a little while Miss Sullivan slowly spelled into my hand the word "d-o-l-l." I was at once interested in this finger play and tried to imitate it. When I finally succeeded in making the letters correctly I was flushed with childish pleasure and pride. Running downstairs to my mother I held up my hand and made the letters for doll. I did not know that I was spelling a word or even that words existed; I was simply making my fingers go in monkey-like imitation. In the days that followed I learned to spell in this uncomprehending way a great many words, among them *pin, hat, cup* and a few verbs like *sit, stand,* and *walk*. But my teacher had been with me several weeks before I understood that everything has a name.

One day, while I was playing with my new doll, Miss Sullivan put a rag doll into my lap, also spelled "d-o-l-l," and tried to make me understand that "d-o-l-l" applied to both. Earlier in the day we had a tussle over the words "m-u-g" and "w-a-t-e-r." Miss Sullivan had tried to impress it upon me that "m-u-g" is *mug* and "w-a-t-e-r" is *water*, but I persisted in confusing the two. In despair she had dropped the subject for the time, only to renew it at the first opportunity. I became impatient at her repeated attempts and, seizing the new doll, I dashed it upon the floor. I was keenly delighted when I felt the fragments of the broken doll at my feet. Neither sorrow nor regret followed my passionate outburst. I had not loved the doll. In the still, dark world in which I lived there was no strong sentiment of tenderness. I felt my teacher sweep the fragments to one side of the hearth, and I had a sense of satisfaction that the cause of my discomfort was removed. She brought me my hat, and I knew I was going out into the warm sunshine. This thought, if a wordless sensation may be called a thought, made me hop and skip with pleasure.

We walked down the path to the well-house, attracted by the fragrance of the honeysuckle with which it was covered. Someone was drawing water and my teacher placed my hand under the spout. As the cool stream gushed over one hand she spelled into the other the word *water*, first slowly, then rapidly. Suddenly I felt a misty consciousness as of something forgotten—a thrill of returning thought; and somehow the mystery of language was revealed to me. I knew then that "w-a-t-e-r" meant the wonderful cool something that was flowing over my hand. That living word awakened my soul, gave it light, hope, joy, set it free! There were barriers still, it is true, but barriers that could in time be swept away.

I left the well-house eager to learn. Everything had a name, and each name gave birth to a new thought. As we returned to the house, every object which I touched seemed to quiver with life. That was because I saw everything with the strange, new sight that had come to me. On entering the door I remembered the doll I had broken. I felt my way to the hearth and picked up the pieces. I tried vainly to put them together. Then my eyes filled with tears; for I realized what I had done, and for the first time I felt repentance and sorrow.

19 Another good name for this selection is—

F "The Mystery of Language Revealed to Me."
G "The Barriers Still Exist."
H "I'll Never Learn to Communicate."
J "How My Teacher Failed Me."

20 The word in quotation marks at the beginning of the selection was the first word—

A Helen Keller spoke to Miss Sullivan.
B Miss Sullivan spoke to Helen Keller.
C Helen Keller spelled into Miss Sullivan's hand.
D Miss Sullivan spelled into Helen Keller's hand.

21 There is enough information in this selection to show that—

F it is very frustrating to be both blind and deaf.
G children with bad manners are often punished.
H people who take good care of their belongings keep them for a long time.
J it is easier to learn new things when outside.

22 Which words did the author use to mean that language enabled her to understand the world around her?

A "I flushed with childish pleasure."
B "I persisted in confounding the two."
C "My eyes filled with tears."
D "I saw everything with the strange, new sight that had come to me."

23 Helen understood the true meaning of language when—

F she walked into the well-house with Miss Sullivan.
G she threw the doll down and broke it.
H the word *water* was spelled into her hand.
J she ran downstairs to her mother.

24 Why does Helen throw the doll on the floor and break it?

A She doesn't like the doll anymore.
B She is impatient with her lessons.
C She wants to hurt her mother's feelings.
D She wants to play outside.

25 If you wanted to know more about Helen Keller, you should—

F look in the encyclopedia under "water."
G read a book about famous people who are blind and deaf.
H visit a doll museum.
J ask a person with a well-house.

26 What is the first lesson Miss Sullivan tries to teach Helen Keller?

_____
_____
_____
_____

Anyone Can Cook!

A cookbook of easy-to-make recipes that taste good and are good for you.

Just learning your way around the kitchen? Want some recipes that are easy to follow and quick to satisfy your sweet tooth? This cookbook is the one for you! And your parents will love it too! The recipes have been approved by the American Nutrition Association. The recipes are low-fat, high-taste.

Anyone Can Cook! comes with 200 recipes, full-color photographs of the finished products, and suggestions for setting the table for special occasions. The cookbook also helps you make grocery lists for the ingredients you will need for the recipes you want to try.

The cookbook has enough recipes and other ideas to help you prepare a completely balanced meal and surprise your family.

The cookbook will help you make and keep friends. Practice the recipes on your friends. They will be delighted! They'll want to help you with your creations.

For a limited time, we are offering *Anyone Can Cook!* for a fantastic price—$12.95 each or 2 for $20.95. And if you order within the next ten days, we will also send you <u>(FREE)</u> a complete set of measuring spoons and cups for each book ordered!!! Don't delay.

To order *Anyone Can Cook!*, just fill out the order form below. Please include a check.

Order Form

- Send me ____ copy(ies) of *Anyone Can Cook!*.
- Also send me _____ <u>**FREE**</u> set(s) of measuring spoons and cups.
- I have enclosed $___.___

Please send my cookbook(s) to:
Name_____
Address_____
City_____State_____Zip_____
Phone (including Area Code) _____

Cut out the order form and mail it to:
Anyone Can Cook!
1012 Cookie Dough Lane
Baking, PA 09876

Allow 4 to 5 weeks for delivery.

27 According to the advertisement, when you practice the recipes on your friends, they will—

A want to help you make your creations.

B not have room to eat dinner at home.

C look for their favorite cookbook at home.

D invite you over to try their favorite creations.

28 All of these are required on the order form except your—

F identification number.

G area code.

H zip code.

J address.

29 To get a free set of measuring spoons and cups you must—

A pay for the cookbook with cash.

B order within ten days.

C fill out the order form.

D buy two copies of the cookbook.

30 The ad tries to interest you in ordering the cookbook by—

F making it sound like fun to make the recipes.

G offering to send you a free copy.

H showing you photographs from the book.

J selling the book through the mail.

31 How long will it take to receive your cookbook?

A 2 to 3 weeks

B 3 to 4 weeks

C 4 to 5 weeks

D 5 to 6 weeks

32 Why would you buy the *Anyone Can Cook!* cookbook?

_____

_____

_____

_____

Answers
27 Ⓐ Ⓑ Ⓒ Ⓓ   28 Ⓕ Ⓖ Ⓗ Ⓙ   29 Ⓐ Ⓑ Ⓒ Ⓓ   30 Ⓕ Ⓖ Ⓗ Ⓙ   31 Ⓐ Ⓑ Ⓒ Ⓓ

Sample A   New From Old

Have you ever wondered what happens to the smashed-up cars you see in junkyards? Old plastic bumpers are recycled and used to make taillight housings for new cars. The metal from old cars are recycled and used for new parts on cars.

According to the selection, how are old plastic bumpers recycled?

A They are used to make trash cans.

B They are molded into milk cartons.

C They are used to make taillight housings for new cars.

D They are molded into playground equipment.

The Game of Water Polo

Do you like to swim and play basketball? Then water polo may be the game for you. Water polo originated in England in the 1870s. It is the oldest team sport played in the Olympics.

The object of water polo is to throw or push a ball into a goal that is about ten feet wide and three feet above the water level. The hollow rubber ball is similar to a volleyball. One point is awarded to the team scoring a goal. Water polo is played in pools about 65 feet wide and 98 feet long. The water depth is about 6 feet. As a result, players must be good swimmers.

A water polo team consists of seven players—a goalie and six field players. Both teams line up on opposite ends of a pool to start a game. A referee tosses the ball into the center of the pool and both teams race for the ball. The ball is moved by players passing it or swimming (also known as dribbling) with it. Field players can have only one hand on the ball at a time. The goalie is allowed to use both hands on the ball. Once a team has the ball, they must take a shot within 35 seconds or they lose possession of the ball.

1 How is the ball moved in water polo?

_____

_____

_____

_____

2 You can conclude from the selection that —

A few people play water polo.

B water polo is less dangerous than basketball.

C water polo is played in many countries in the world.

D fouls seldom occur in water polo.

Answers
SA Ⓐ Ⓑ Ⓒ Ⓓ   2 Ⓐ Ⓑ Ⓒ Ⓓ

Soccer: From Past to Present

People have been playing soccer for hundreds of years. The ancient Chinese and Romans played a game similar to soccer. In London, children played a form of the game in the 1100s. The sport was introduced to the United States by immigrants in the early 1800s. Today soccer has become quite popular in the United States.

Soccer is played on a field just about the size of a football field. Goals, set at each end of the field, are the targets of the game. The players use a lightweight leather ball.

The rules of the game are fairly simple. Eleven players participate on each team. A team gains points each time a player kicks or hits the ball into the other team's goal. The only player on each team who is permitted to catch and throw the ball is the goalkeeper, who is assigned to protect the goal. The other players cannot catch the ball with their hands. They are allowed to kick it, bounce it off their heads, or block it with their bodies.

Soccer is one of the most popular games in the world. Many children begin playing soccer at an early age. High schools and colleges have soccer teams. Many countries have professional teams, whose players are paid for their full-time participation. They also have *semiprofessional* teams, whose members participate and are paid on a part-time basis.

One reason for the popularity of soccer is that it is relatively inexpensive to buy equipment for soccer teams. Perhaps the best thing about soccer is that players do not have to be a certain height, age, or weight. Soccer is a team sport that requires speed and cooperation. Soccer is a game for everyone.

3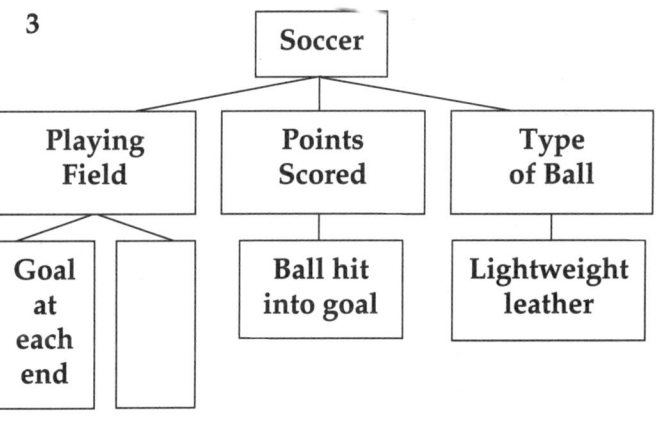

The web shows some ideas discussed in the article. Which of these belongs in the empty box?

F size of football field

G ancient Chinese and Roman

H bounce off heads

J certain height and age

4 In this article, *semiprofessional* means—

A paid on a full-time basis.

B not paid.

C not paid on a full-time basis.

D paid once a year.

5 When was soccer first introduced to the United States?

_____

_____

_____

_____

Answers
3 Ⓕ Ⓖ Ⓗ Ⓙ   4 Ⓐ Ⓑ Ⓒ Ⓓ

A Difficult Decision

Frieda and her mother lived in an apartment in New York City. Frieda had no brothers or sisters, and there were no children living nearby. Her best friend was a very old woman named Maria, who lived down the hall.

Maria's most prized possessions were a cat named Javier and an album of photographs from her family in Costa Rica. When she visited Maria, Frieda liked to study the album. Men in big mustaches and women in blouses *embroidered* with bright flowers, leaves, and native animals stared from the photographs. Maria would begin by talking about these long-dead relatives but would end by telling stories about the jaguars and parrots that lived in the rain forest near her family home. Frieda loved listening to these stories. She wanted to become a scientist to help save the rain forests from destruction.

One night as Frieda was doing her homework she heard sirens, and fire trucks suddenly appeared on the street below. The next thing she knew, a firefighter was pounding on their door. The top floors of the building were on fire. Frieda's mother shouted, "Grab your stereo and let's go!" Frieda had saved her money for a year to buy the stereo.

"Maria may need help," Frieda yelled as she raced down the hall to her friend's apartment. The door was standing open. The firefighters had already helped Maria and Javier downstairs. Frieda grabbed the heavy photo album from the shelf where Maria always kept it. Frieda hurried downstairs; smoke was filling the hallways.

Frieda's mother was anxiously waiting for her on the street. She saw that her daughter had saved only Maria's photo album. "I'm sorry about your stereo," Frieda's mother said.

"That's all right," Frieda said, "I made the right choice."

6 According to the story, Frieda grabbed the photo album mainly because—

F she knew it meant a lot to Maria.
G she always wanted to own it.
H she did not see anything else to save.
J Maria told her to save it.

7 The story takes place in—

A Costa Rica.
B the country.
C a tropical rain forest.
D New York City.

8 Maria's most prized possessions were an album of photographs and a—

F collection of postcards.
G parrot from Brazil.
H a cat named Javier.
J a grandfather clock.

9 This selection is mostly about a girl who—

A fights a fire.
B saves her own favorite thing.
C knows how to save money.
D makes a difficult choice.

10 Why did Frieda want to become a scientist?

F to find a cure for cancer
G to become rich and famous
H to have a better life for herself and her mother
J to save the rain forests from destruction

11 Which statement is an opinion in the story?

A The top floors of the building were on fire.
B Frieda had no brothers or sisters.
C Frieda made the right choice.
D The firefighters helped Maria and Javier downstairs.

12 Which of these sentences would fit best at the end of this story?

F "My album cost more than the stereo."
G "I will give her a reward."
H "I am tired of my stereo."
J "I could never replace the album."

13 In order to answer question 12, the best thing to do is—

A reread the first sentence of each paragraph.
B think about the entire story.
C look for the words "stereo and album."
D analyze the picture that goes with the story.

14 In this story, *embroidered* means—

F decorated with fancy raised designs made with thread.
G dry-clean only.
H made in Costa Rica.
J smooth-textured, imported fabric.

15 Why did Frieda like to visit Maria?

_____
_____
_____
_____

DON'T BE LEFT IN THE DUST!

Make others eat *YOUR* dust.

Buy

DUST BUSTERS RUNNING SHOES.

Run faster, Run farther, Run forever!

Our shoes are the best running shoes on the market.
Chances are that 5 out of 6 runners wear our shoes.
You won't know for sure—those wearing our shoes can never be caught.

- **Dust Busters Running Shoes** come in over 95 sizes—fit for ALL!

- Our shoes are all leather uppers with rubber soles.

- Our shoes offer extra support in the ankles and heels to prevent injury.

- Our shoes come with a money-back guarantee good for 5 years.

SO, WALK—NO, JOG—ON SECOND THOUGHT, RUN to your nearest shoe store.

You'll never eat dust again. We promise!

GO FOR THE GOLD!

No one wants to be second best.

Go for the GOLD! Buy **FINISH FIRST** running shoes.

■ We guarantee you will WIN EVERY RACE if you wear our shoes.

■ The design of our shoes is the LATEST SPORTS FASHION. The shoes are streamlined to avoid any extra weight on your feet. This lightens the load giving you the EDGE YOU NEED TO WIN!

■ The soles of the shoes have ridges that help your feet grip the track. NO MORE SLIPPING.

■ Air holes, scientifically positioned LET YOUR FEET BREATHE.

KEEP AHEAD OF THE PACK.

GO FOR THE GOLD!

16 You would most likely find these ads in a—

A hardware store sales flyer.

B sports magazine.

C telephone book.

D road atlas.

17 The Finish First ad stresses the shoes'—

F streamlined design.

G variety of sizes.

H rubber soles.

J leather uppers.

18 In the Finish First ad, the words "Go for the GOLD!" mean—

A look for money.

B race to win.

C choose your color.

D find a partner.

19 What material is used to make the upper part of the Dust Busters shoe?

F rubber

G leather

H plastic

J The ad does not say.

20 Which of these is an opinion in the Dust Busters shoe ad?

A Dust Busters running shoes come in over 95 sizes.

B Our shoes come with a money-back guarantee good for 5 years.

C Our shoes offer extra support in the ankles and heels.

D Our shoes are the best running shoes on the market.

21 Why is there extra support in the ankles and heels?

_____

_____

_____

_____

Answers
16 Ⓐ Ⓑ Ⓒ Ⓓ   17 Ⓕ Ⓖ Ⓗ Ⓙ   18 Ⓐ Ⓑ Ⓒ Ⓓ   19 Ⓕ Ⓖ Ⓗ Ⓙ   20 Ⓐ Ⓑ Ⓒ Ⓓ

A Man of Many Talents

Thomas Jefferson was the third President of the United States. He is also well-known for many other achievements. He was a writer, an architect, an inventor, and a music lover.

Jefferson was involved in government for many years before he became President. He was the governor of Virginia, a U.S. congressman, the minister to France, and the Vice President of the United States. He helped to write the Declaration of Independence, the Constitution, and the Bill of Rights.

Jefferson served as President from 1801 to 1809. Many changes occurred during his time in office. He tried to keep government simple and began to reduce government spending and to cut taxes. In 1803, the United States bought the Louisiana Territory from France. This territory nearly doubled the size of the country. He asked two army officers and explorers, Lewis and Clark, to travel through the new land and find out all about it.

During and after his time as President, Jefferson followed his other interests. He designed Monticello, his Virginia home, and the Virginia Capitol building. He invented the swivel chair and the dumbwaiter.

Jefferson contributed greatly to the development of the University of Virginia. In addition to designing the university buildings, he planned the courses, hired the teachers, and selected the books. The university opened its doors in 1825.

Jefferson was a man of many talents, and he used his talents to improve life for many people in his country.

---

22 This article is most like—

F a folk tale.

G historical fiction.

H a biography.

J fantasy.

23 There is enough information in this article to show that Thomas Jefferson—

A was a good musician and a talented singer.

B paid too much money for the Louisiana Territory.

C greatly contributed to his country and its people.

D increased government spending and increased taxes.

24 To learn more about Thomas Jefferson you should—

F visit Louisiana.

G look in a book about Presidents of the United States.

H go to a university in France.

J look in the dictionary under "architect."

25 What are some of the things Thomas Jefferson is known for?

_____
_____
_____
_____

Answers
22 Ⓕ Ⓖ Ⓗ Ⓙ   23 Ⓐ Ⓑ Ⓒ Ⓓ   24 Ⓕ Ⓖ Ⓗ Ⓙ

UNIT FOUR
Reading Vocabulary

Determining Word Meanings

Directions: Darken the circle, or write the answer, for the word or group of words that has the same or almost the same meaning as the underlined word.

TRY THIS Choose your answer carefully. The other choices may seem correct. Be sure to think about the meaning of the underlined word.

Sample A

Collapsed means—

A fell down
B went up
C sold out
D blew up

THINK IT THROUGH The correct answer is A. Collapsed means "fell down." Collapsed does not mean "went up," "sold out," or "blew up."

---

1 To grieve is to—
   A donate
   B wonder
   C celebrate
   D mourn

2 To be vertical is to be—
   F leaning
   G straight up and down
   H straight across
   J broken

3 Something that is frequent is—
   A occurring seldom
   B a holiday
   C happening often
   D sad

4 To evaluate is to—
   F judge
   G honor
   H destroy
   J create

5 To capsize is to—
   A load
   B get out of
   C overturn
   D launch

6 An image is—
   F an intention
   G a picture
   H a subject
   J a fact

7 Final is the same as—
   A last
   B first
   C important
   D most exciting

8 What is another word that means the same as accused?

   _____
   _____
   _____
   _____
   _____

Answers
SA Ⓐ Ⓑ Ⓒ Ⓓ   2 Ⓕ Ⓖ Ⓗ Ⓙ   4 Ⓕ Ⓖ Ⓗ Ⓙ   6 Ⓕ Ⓖ Ⓗ Ⓙ
1 Ⓐ Ⓑ Ⓒ Ⓓ   3 Ⓐ Ⓑ Ⓒ Ⓓ   5 Ⓐ Ⓑ Ⓒ Ⓓ   7 Ⓐ Ⓑ Ⓒ Ⓓ

Matching Words with More Than One Meaning

Directions: Darken the circle, or write the answer, for the sentence that uses the underlined word in the same way as the sentence in the box.

 Read the sentence in the box. Decide what the underlined word means. Then find the sentence in which the underlined word has the same meaning.

Sample A

> He cut his head when he fell.

In which sentence does head have the same meaning as it does in the sentence above?

A Stand at the head of the stairs.
B She laid her head on her arm.
C Did you buy a head of lettuce?
D She owns forty head of cattle.

THINK IT THROUGH The correct answer is B. In choice B and in the sentence in the box, head means "a part of your body."

---

1. > I wrote a check for the groceries.

    In which sentence does check have the same meaning as it does in the sentence above?

    A Melissa had to check her urge to laugh during the concert.
    B The teacher will check the answers.
    C Mom paid my fee with a check.
    D You need to check your calculations.

2. > Ann trimmed the collar with lace.

    In which sentence does lace have the same meaning as it does in the sentence above?

    F The little boy tries to lace his shoes.
    G Marissa bought a yard of lace for the dress she is making.
    H They stopped the game while the girl tied her shoe lace.
    J Dad will lace the drink with green food coloring.

3. > Each hall monitor is required to wear a name tag.

    In which sentence does monitor have the same meaning as it does in the sentence above?

    A Can you see the computer monitor?
    B A monitor in the hospital room kept track of his heartbeats.
    C The teacher will monitor the student's progress and report it to the parents.
    D Is she the classroom monitor today?

4. > She used a tissue to dry her eyes.

    Use tissue in a sentence where it has the same meaning as in the sentence above.

    _____
    _____
    _____
    _____

Answers
SA Ⓐ Ⓑ Ⓒ Ⓓ   1 Ⓐ Ⓑ Ⓒ Ⓓ   2 Ⓕ Ⓖ Ⓗ Ⓙ   3 Ⓐ Ⓑ Ⓒ Ⓓ

Using Context Clues

Directions: Darken the circle, or write the answer, for the word or words that give the meaning of the underlined word.

TRY THIS Read the first sentence carefully. Look for clue words in the sentence. Then use each answer choice in place of the underlined word. Be sure that your answer and the underlined word have the same meaning.

Sample A

We were surprised by the principal's unexpected announcement. Unexpected means—

A long
B planned
C sudden
D last

THINK IT THROUGH The correct answer is C. Unexpected means "sudden." The clue word is "surprised."

---

1. There is some kind of obstacle blocking the highway. Obstacle means—

   A a truck
   B a traffic jam
   C an accident
   D a barrier

2. Events that are organized rarely have any last-minute problems. Organized means—

   F in order
   G dissolved
   H exciting
   J educational

3. Our food supplies were dwindling steadily. Dwindling means—

   A increasing
   B rotting
   C shrinking
   D improving

4. The people were eager for the opera to commence. Commence means—

   F conclude
   G begin
   H continue
   J close

5. When metal rusts it becomes tarnished. Tarnished means—

   A brittle
   B soft
   C strengthened
   D discolored

6. The reckless driver finally came to a stop when he crashed into the building. What does reckless mean?

   _____
   _____
   _____
   _____

Answers

SA Ⓐ Ⓑ Ⓒ Ⓓ   2 Ⓕ Ⓖ Ⓗ Ⓙ   4 Ⓕ Ⓖ Ⓗ Ⓙ
1 Ⓐ Ⓑ Ⓒ Ⓓ   3 Ⓐ Ⓑ Ⓒ Ⓓ   5 Ⓐ Ⓑ Ⓒ Ⓓ

49

Test

Sample A

To <u>astonish</u> is to—

A decrease
B calm
C awaken
D amaze

For questions 1–8, darken the circle for the word or group of words that has the same or almost the same meaning as the underlined word.

1 <u>Abruptly</u> means—
   A suddenly
   B slowly
   C tearfully
   D angrily

2 <u>Sincerely</u> means—
   F softly
   G honestly
   H angrily
   J loudly

3 To <u>neglect</u> is to—
   A ignore
   B mold
   C restrain
   D behold

4 To be <u>incomplete</u> is to be—
   F incorrect
   G unfinished
   H final
   J difficult

5 A <u>conversation</u> is a—
   A smile
   B quality
   C discussion
   D solution

6 To <u>expand</u> means to—
   F tumble
   G divide
   H assign
   J swell

7 <u>Triple</u> means—
   A three times
   B double
   C six times
   D four times

8 To be <u>urgent</u> is to be—
   F ideal
   G simple
   H important
   J abundant

Write your answer for the following question:

9 If something is <u>fake</u>, it's—

_____
_____
_____
_____

Answers
SA Ⓐ Ⓑ Ⓒ Ⓓ   2 Ⓕ Ⓖ Ⓗ Ⓙ   4 Ⓕ Ⓖ Ⓗ Ⓙ   6 Ⓕ Ⓖ Ⓗ Ⓙ   8 Ⓕ Ⓖ Ⓗ Ⓙ
1 Ⓐ Ⓑ Ⓒ Ⓓ   3 Ⓐ Ⓑ Ⓒ Ⓓ   5 Ⓐ Ⓑ Ⓒ Ⓓ   7 Ⓐ Ⓑ Ⓒ Ⓓ

Sample B

> Don't try to jam the book into that little space on the shelf.

In which sentence does jam have the same meaning as it does in the sentence above?

A Aunt Harriet's homemade peach jam is delicious.

B We won't jam too many people into the elevator.

C He had to jam on the brakes to avoid a crash.

D Be careful not to jam your finger playing ball.

For questions 10–13, darken the circle for the sentence that uses the underlined word in the same way as the sentence in the box.

10
> Meredith operates a crane at the shipyard.

In which sentence does crane have the same meaning as it does in the sentence above?

A The crane lifted huge crates.

B The photographer approached the young crane at the water's edge.

C Don't crane your neck to see the film.

D We want to see the crane at the zoo.

11
> The stock market fell yesterday in light trading.

In which sentence does stock have the same meaning as it does in the sentence above?

F They will stock the river with trout.

G Chicken stock is the base for many soups.

H She bought some stock as an investment.

J You need to stock up on canned goods.

12
> Turn up the volume so we can hear the announcement.

In which sentence does volume have the same meaning as it does in the sentence above?

A The volume of the container was too small and the water spilled out.

B Which volume of the encyclopedia are you using?

C This is just one volume that the library owns.

D Play the CD player at full volume.

13
> Don't make a rash decision that you might regret later.

In which sentence does rash have the same meaning as it does in the sentence above?

F How did you get that rash on your arm?

G Mandy made a rash judgment about the new girl in her class.

H The store received a rash of complaints from the customers.

J A side effect of the medicine is a rash.

Write your answer for the following question:

14
> I thought her attitude was very negative.

Use negative in a sentence where it has a different meaning than in the sentence above.

_____
_____
_____
_____

Sample C

Will you put your dirty clothes in the <u>hamper</u>? <u>Hamper</u> means—

A room
B bag
C basket
D washer

For questions 15–21, darken the circle for the word or words that give the meaning of the underlined word.

15 She bought fresh <u>produce</u> to use in her meal. <u>Produce</u> means—

A yield
B vegetables
C make
D show

16 It is <u>customary</u> for politicians running for office to make promises. <u>Customary</u> means—

F unusual
G unexpected
H uncommon
J usual

17 Ann's mother was excited about getting a job <u>promotion</u>. <u>Promotion</u> means—

A demotion
B description
C advancement
D notice

18 The <u>triumphant</u> team paraded around the field after the game. <u>Triumphant</u> means—

F victorious
G solemn
H sad
J defeated

19 Large-scale <u>commerce</u> is necessary for economic development. <u>Commerce</u> means—

A conversation
B buying
C selling
D business

20 They went to a health <u>resort</u> for the weekend. <u>Resort</u> means—

F spa
G chance
H hope
J store

21 A computer software company will <u>occupy</u> the top floor. <u>Occupy</u> means—

A inhabit
B lease
C inherit
D analyze

Write your answer for the following question:

22 You should trace the <u>figure</u> on your paper. What is another word that means <u>figure</u>?

_____

_____

_____

_____

UNIT FIVE
Math Problem-Solving Strategies

Overview

The Problem-Solving Plan

When solving math problems follow these steps:

STEP 1: WHAT IS THE QUESTION/GOAL?

Decide what must be found. This information is usually presented in the form of a question.

STEP 2: FIND THE FACTS

Locate the factual information in three different ways:
- A. KEY FACTS...the facts you need to solve the problem.
- B. FACTS YOU DON'T NEED...those facts which are not necessary for solving the problem.
- C. ARE MORE FACTS NEEDED?...decide if you have enough information to solve the problem.

STEP 3: SELECT A STRATEGY

Decide what strategies you might use, how you will use them, and then estimate what your answer will be. If one strategy doesn't help you to solve the problem, try another.

STEP 4: SOLVE

Apply the strategy according to your plan. Use an operation if necessary, and clearly indicate your answer.

STEP 5: DOES YOUR RESPONSE MAKE SENSE?

Check to make sure that your answer makes sense. Use estimation or approximation strategies.

Problem 1

PROBLEM/QUESTION:

Joey worked at a camp for the summer. He worked 6 hours each day for 42 days and earned $12 each day. If Joey was paid $3.00 for each hour he worked instead of $12 per day, would he earn more or less money?

STEP 1: WHAT IS THE QUESTION/GOAL?

STEP 2: FIND THE FACTS

STEP 3: SELECT A STRATEGY

STEP 4: SOLVE

STEP 5: DOES YOUR RESPONSE MAKE SENSE?

Problem 2

PROBLEM/QUESTION:

Rosa walked to her friend's house, which was 12 blocks away. It took her 20 minutes. The return trip took an extra 10 minutes because she stopped for ice cream, which added 4 blocks to her trip. Draw a map that shows her trip and indicate the time it took.

STEP 1: WHAT IS THE QUESTION/GOAL?

STEP 2: FIND THE FACTS

STEP 3: SELECT A STRATEGY

STEP 4: SOLVE

STEP 5: DOES YOUR RESPONSE MAKE SENSE?

UNIT SIX
Math Problem Solving

Understanding Number Relationships

Directions: Darken the circle for the correct answer, or write it in the space provided.

TRY THIS — Read each question carefully. Decide the best method to solve the problem. Make sure you understand the question that is being asked.

Sample A

Marla's most recent recorded times for the 100-meter dash were: 12.1 seconds, 12.08 seconds, 12.2 seconds, and 12.33 seconds. Which shows the times listed from fastest to slowest?

A 12.2, 12.1, 12.08, 12.33
B 12.33, 12.1, 12.08, 12.2
C 12.08, 12.1, 12.2, 12.33
D 12.08, 12.33, 12.2, 12.1

THINK IT THROUGH — The correct answer is C. First, look at the number in the tenths column. Next, look at the hundredths column.

---

1. Each square represents 0.01. What decimal number is shown below?

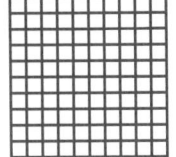

A 1.56
B 16.6
C 15.6
D 1.66

2. Which decimal shows the part of the figure that is shaded?

F 0.29
G 0.28
H 0.35
J 0.72

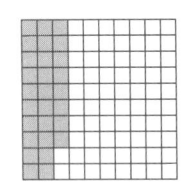

3. Write $\frac{38}{6}$ as a mixed number.

_____

4.
Trail mix (Makes six 8 oz. servings)	
2 cups raisins	$\frac{1}{2}$ cup walnuts
$2\frac{1}{2}$ cups peanuts	$1\frac{3}{4}$ cups dried fruit
$\frac{1}{2}$ cup sunflower seeds	$\frac{1}{4}$ cup shredded coconut

Which ingredient is used in the greatest quantity in the trail mix?

A raisins   C peanuts
B coconut   D dried fruit

5. How is 2,401,226,000 written in words?

F two million, four hundred one thousand, two hundred twenty-six

G two billion, four hundred one million, two hundred twenty-six thousand

H two billion, four hundred ten million, two hundred twenty six thousand

J twenty-four billion, one million, two hundred twenty-six thousand

---

Answers
SA Ⓐ Ⓑ Ⓒ Ⓓ   2 Ⓕ Ⓖ Ⓗ Ⓙ   5 Ⓕ Ⓖ Ⓗ Ⓙ
1   Ⓐ Ⓑ Ⓒ Ⓓ   4 Ⓐ Ⓑ Ⓒ Ⓓ

Understanding Number Theory

Directions: Darken the circle for the correct answer, or write it in the space provided.

> **TRY THIS** Read each question carefully. Work the problem on scratch paper. Try each answer choice in the problem before you choose your answer.

Sample A

What number is shown here?

200,000 + 50,000 + 70 + 8

- A 25,078
- B 205,708
- C 250,078
- D 20,578

> **THINK IT THROUGH** The correct answer is C. Add up the numbers as shown to get the answer.
>
>   200,000
>   50,000
>   70
> +   8

---

1 What is the value of the 6 in 45.261?

- A 6 tenths
- B 6 hundredths
- C 6 thousandths
- D 6 tens

2 What is the minimum number of cookies Margie would have to bake in order to divide the cookies equally among her 6 neighborhood friends with none left over or among her 24 classmates with none left over?

- F 12
- G 16
- H 24
- J 30

3 What is the greatest common factor of 40 and 24?

- A 4
- B 8
- C 12
- D 48

4 These beads represent the number 125,306,987. What place value is represented with three beads?

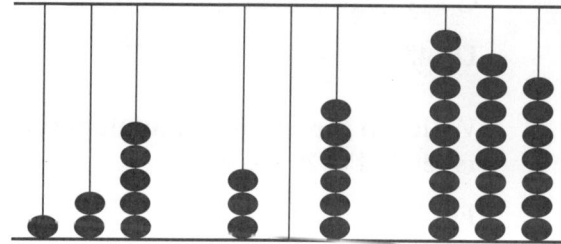

- F thousands
- G ten thousands
- H hundred thousands
- J millions

5 An airport runway measures 2,300 meters long. How long will the runway be if it is increased by 2,000 meters?

_____

_____

_____

_____

Answers
SA Ⓐ Ⓑ Ⓒ Ⓓ   1 Ⓐ Ⓑ Ⓒ Ⓓ   2 Ⓕ Ⓖ Ⓗ Ⓙ   3 Ⓐ Ⓑ Ⓒ Ⓓ   4 Ⓕ Ⓖ Ⓗ Ⓙ

Working with Algebra

Directions: Darken the circle for the correct answer, or write it in the space provided.

TRY THIS Check your work by making sure both sides of an equation are equal values. Try using all the answer choices back in the problem.

Sample A

If $y + 13 = 25$, what number replaces the y to make the sentence true?

A 6   C 15
B 12   D 38

THINK IT THROUGH The correct answer is B. Change + 13 to − 13 and move it to the right side of the equation. Subtract from 25 to get the value of y.

---

1 If $x + 14 = 33$, what is the value of x?

A 11
B 15
C 19
D 47

2 Which of the following number sentences is related to $20 \div 4 = n$?

F $4 \times \square = 20$
G $4 \times 20 = \square$
H $20 - 4 = \square$
J $4 \div \square = 20$

3 Which expression shows that 12 less than x equals 40?

A $x - 12 = 40$
B $12 - x = 40$
C $12 \div x = 40$
D $40 - 12 \leq x$

4 Which number sentence is related to $8 + 3 = 11$?

F $8 \times 3 = 24$ H $5 + 6 = 11$
G $11 - 3 = 8$ J $8 - 11 = 3$

5 There are 4 sixth-grade teachers at Emerson Middle School. Each teacher has 23 students. These teachers will give 2 worksheets to every student. Which number sentence would be used to find W, the total number of worksheets needed?

A $(23 \div 4) + 2 = W$
B $2 + (4 + 23) = W$
C $(4 \times 23) \times 2 = W$
D $23 + (2 \times 4) = W$

6 Each rack at the bowling alley holds 18 bowling balls. There are 6 racks on each of 3 walls. Write a number sentence to find B, the total number of bowling balls that the racks can hold.

_____
_____
_____
_____

Answers

SA Ⓐ Ⓑ Ⓒ Ⓓ   2 Ⓕ Ⓖ Ⓗ Ⓙ   4 Ⓕ Ⓖ Ⓗ Ⓙ
1 Ⓐ Ⓑ Ⓒ Ⓓ   3 Ⓐ Ⓑ Ⓒ Ⓓ   5 Ⓐ Ⓑ Ⓒ Ⓓ

Working with Probability and Statistics

Directions: Darken the circle for the correct answer, or write it in the space provided.

> **TRY THIS** Read each problem carefully. Look for key words or numbers in the question that tell you what to look for in the graph or table.

Sample A

Each letter in the word *mathematics* is written on a card and placed in a box. If Keiko chooses a card without looking, what is the probability that she will choose the letter *t*.

A $\frac{1}{11}$ C $\frac{3}{11}$
B $\frac{2}{11}$ D $\frac{4}{11}$

> **THINK IT THROUGH** The correct answer is <u>B</u>. There are 2 Ts in the word mathematics, which contains 11 letters. The probability of choosing the letter T is expressed as $\frac{2}{11}$.

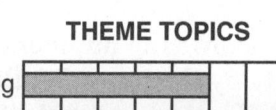

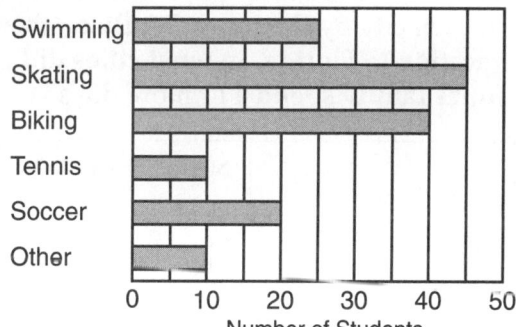

1. How many more students wrote about biking than about tennis?

   A 30 students   C 40 students
   B 50 students   D 10 students

2. The school cafeteria sells sandwiches on whole wheat or white bread, made with turkey, beef, chicken, or tuna fish. How many different sandwich combinations are possible?

   F 2   H 6
   G 4   J 8

3. Hal planned to buy a new shirt. The store had red, white, and blue shirts. Each color was available with or without a pocket, in short sleeves or long sleeves. How many different combinations did Hal have to choose from?

   A 7   C 12
   B 10   D 14

4. It is Tonya's turn in a board game she is playing with her family. Why is there a greater probability that Tonya will go back 2 spaces than move ahead 2 spaces?

   _____
   _____
   _____
   _____
   _____
   _____
   _____

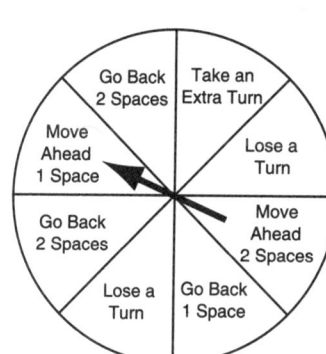

Answers
SA Ⓐ Ⓑ Ⓒ Ⓓ   1 Ⓐ Ⓑ Ⓒ Ⓓ   2 Ⓕ Ⓖ Ⓗ Ⓙ   3 Ⓐ Ⓑ Ⓒ Ⓓ

5. According to the graph, what was the average number of cars sold by the four dealerships in one year?

Number of Cars Sold in 1 Year

Car City	🚗🚗🚗🚗🚗
Downtown Motors	🚗🚗🚗🚗🚗🚗
Smith's Car Emporium	🚗🚗🚗
Carver Car Sales	🚗🚗🚗🚗🚗

Each 🚗 = 100 cars

F 445
G 475
H 525
J 1,900

The students in Mrs. O'Brien's art classes completed their projects last month. The graph shows the kinds of projects the students made. Use the graph to answer questions 6 and 7.

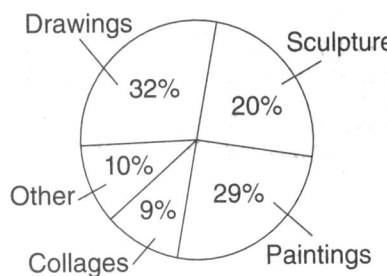

6. If 500 art projects were completed, how many were drawings?

A 32
B 160
C 468
D 532

7. What fraction of the projects was made up of sculpture?

F $\frac{1}{20}$
G $\frac{1}{16}$
H $\frac{1}{10}$
J $\frac{1}{5}$

8. According to the table shown here, which two cities together receive a total of 72 inches of rain per year?

Texas City	Rain Per Year
Austin	30 inches
Dallas	35 inches
El Paso	8 inches
Fort Worth	35 inches
Houston	42 inches

A Austin and Dallas
B Dallas and El Paso
C Fort Worth and Dallas
D Austin and Houston

9. This chart shows the number of days spent in each city by the Jones family on their vacation to Florida. In what cities did the Jones family spend 4 or more days?

City	Number of Days
Miami	|||
Ft. Lauderdale	||
Orlando	|||| |||
Tampa	||||
Naples	||||

_____
_____
_____
_____
_____
_____

Understanding Geometry

Directions: Darken the circle for the correct answer, or write the answer in the space provided.

TRY THIS Read each question carefully. Use the objects shown to help you answer each question. Remember that perimeter is the measurement around the outside, while area is the measurement of the inside of a space.

Sample A

Which line segment is a radius of this circle?

A $\overline{AC}$
B $\overline{PB}$
C $\overline{AB}$
D $\overline{CA}$

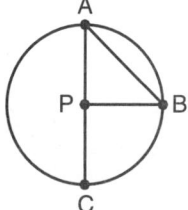

THINK IT THROUGH The correct answer is <u>B</u>. A radius is a line segment that connects the center with the outside of the circle.

---

1 In the circle shown here, C is the center. How long is the diameter of the circle?

A 8 inches
B 16 inches
C 3.14 inches
D 4 inches

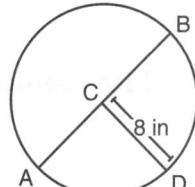

2 Name the coordinates of point B on the grid shown here.

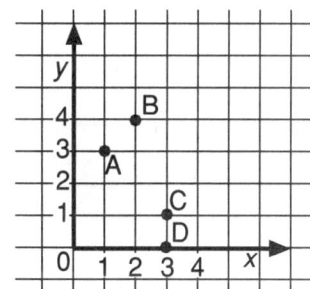

F (1, 3)
G (2, 4)
H (3, 1)
J (4, 2)

3 Which slice of pie forms a right angle?

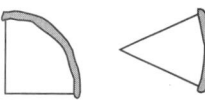
   A   B   C   D

A A
B B
C C
D D

4 Which figure does <u>not</u> show a line of symmetry?

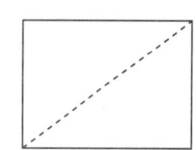 F
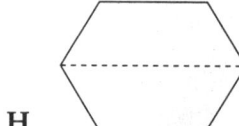 H

 G
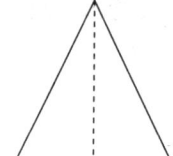 J

Answers
SA Ⓐ Ⓑ Ⓒ Ⓓ   1 Ⓐ Ⓑ Ⓒ Ⓓ   2 Ⓕ Ⓖ Ⓗ Ⓙ   3 Ⓐ Ⓑ Ⓒ Ⓓ   4 Ⓕ Ⓖ Ⓗ Ⓙ

5 Use your inch ruler to help you answer this question. What is the perimeter of the triangle shown here?

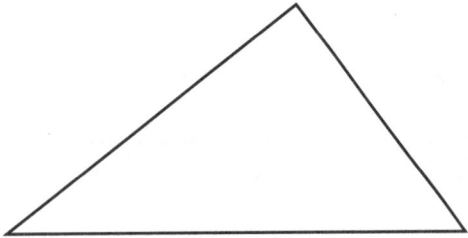

A $4\frac{1}{2}$ in.
B $5\frac{3}{4}$ in.
C 6 in.
D 7 in.

6 Use your centimeter ruler to help you answer this question. Which figure shown here has an area of 6 cm²?

F

G

H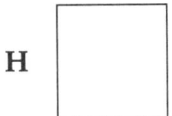

J

7 Which figure shows the result of rotating the tennis shoe 180°?

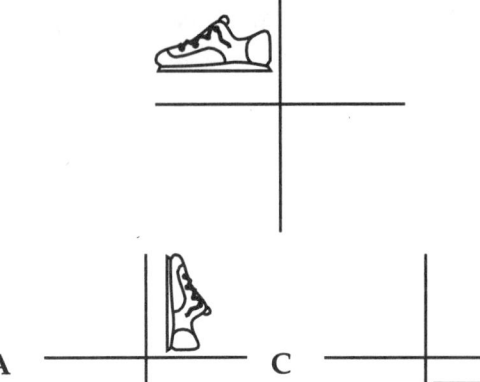

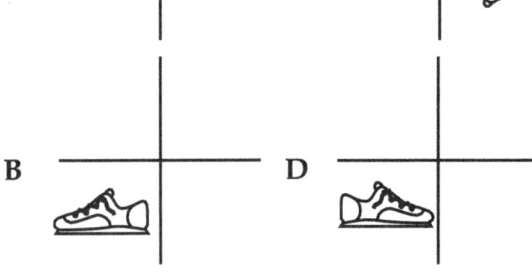

8 Which coordinates represent the location of Midtown University on the map?

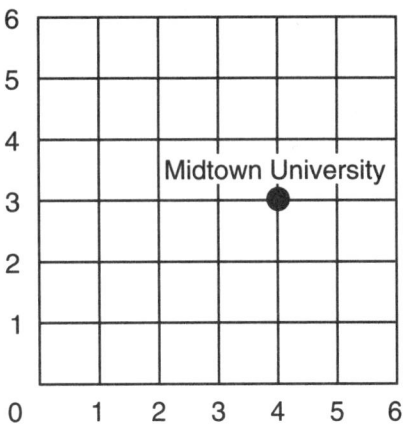

Working with Measurement

Directions: Darken the circle for the correct answer, or write the answer in the space provided.

TRY THIS Read each question carefully. Use the objects shown or named to help you answer each question.

Sample A

Which unit of measurement is best to use to describe the weight of an egg?

A ounces C inches
B liters D yards

THINK IT THROUGH The correct answer is A. Liters are used to measure capacity, and inches and yards are units of linear measurement.

1 What is the area of the shaded section of this figure?

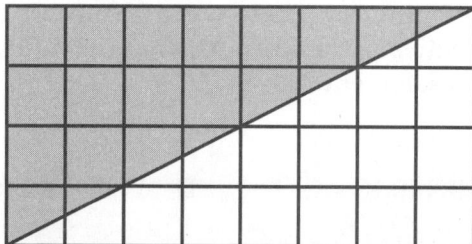

A 20 square units
B 16 square units
C 15 square units
D 12 square units

2 What units are used to measure length on a ruler?

F degrees
G kilograms
H centimeters
J liters

3 Use your inch ruler and the map to help you answer the question. What is the actual distance between the two universities?

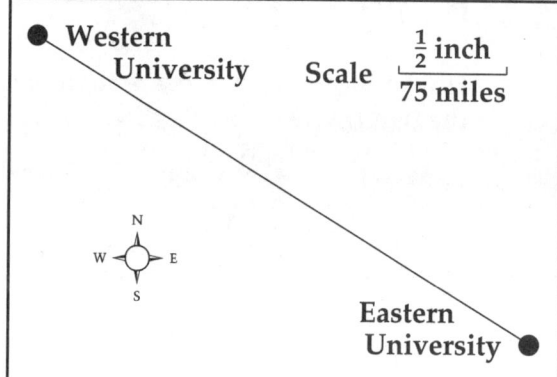

Scale $\frac{1}{2}$ inch / 75 miles

A 150 miles   C 450 miles
B 300 miles   D 600 miles

4 Lilly measured the driveway from the street to the garage. She measured 30 feet. How would you change that measurement to inches?

_____
_____
_____
_____
_____
_____

Answers
SA Ⓐ Ⓑ Ⓒ Ⓓ   1 Ⓐ Ⓑ Ⓒ Ⓓ   2 Ⓕ Ⓖ Ⓗ Ⓙ   3 Ⓐ Ⓑ Ⓒ Ⓓ

63

5 The Marsh family rode their bikes to the state park and back last Saturday. It took 1 hour 40 minutes to ride to the park and 1 hour 55 minutes to ride back home. How long was their trip altogether?

F 4 hours

G 3 hours 35 minutes

H 3 hours 25 minutes

J 2 hours 35 minutes

6 The parade began at 8:45 A.M. If it lasted 2 hours and 30 minutes, at what time did the parade end?

A 10:45 A.M.

B 10:30 A.M.

C 11:15 A.M.

D 11:45 A.M.

7 How many centimeters are there between the two trees?

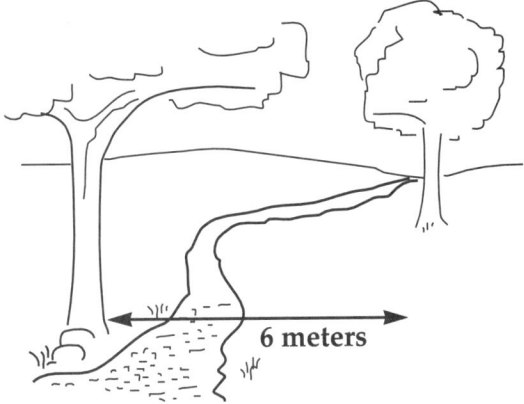

F 6,000 centimeters

G 600 centimeters

H 60 centimeters

J 0.06 centimeters

8 Which of these equals the least amount?

A 4 cups   C 2 quarts

B 3 pints   D 1 gallon

9 A football player kicked a football 45.5 feet. How long was the kick in yards and inches?

F 2 yards 13 inches

G 3 yards 9 inches

H 12 yards 3 inches

J 15 yards 6 inches

10 The testing session began at 8:45 A.M. The time limit on the first test was 35 minutes and the time limit on the second test was 40 minutes. There was a 10-minute break between the tests. At what time did the session end?

A 10:00 A.M.   C 10:25 A.M.

B 10:10 A.M.   D 11:05 A.M.

11 How would you compute the actual distance from the nautical museum to the lighthouse?

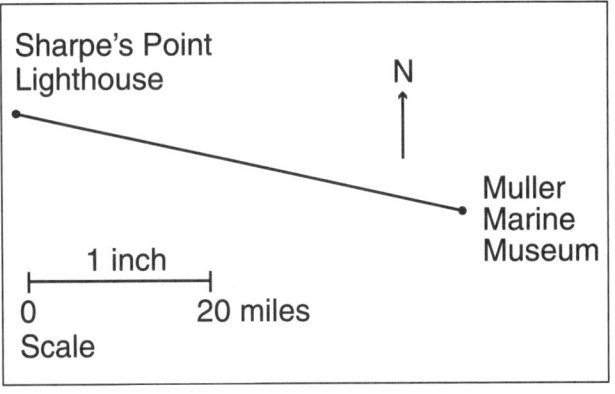

Answers

5 Ⓕ Ⓖ Ⓗ Ⓙ   7 Ⓕ Ⓖ Ⓗ Ⓙ   9 Ⓕ Ⓖ Ⓗ Ⓙ

6 Ⓐ Ⓑ Ⓒ Ⓓ   8 Ⓐ Ⓑ Ⓒ Ⓓ   10 Ⓐ Ⓑ Ⓒ Ⓓ

Understanding Patterns and Functions

Directions: Darken the circle for the correct answer, or write the answer in the space provided.

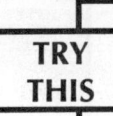 **TRY THIS** — Read each problem carefully. Try to determine the nature of the pattern or the relationship in the problem. Try using all the answer choices back in the problem. Then choose the answer that you think best answers the question.

Sample A

A special machine multiplies any number entered into it by a secret number. The table shows how numbers are changed. Which number is missing from the table?

Original number	6	4	10
New number		20	50

A 50 C 30
B 40 D 15

 **THINK IT THROUGH** — The correct answer is C. Each original number is multiplied by 5 to get the new number.

---

1 Look at the pattern shown here. What number is missing from this number pattern?

101, 105, ____, 113, 117

A 107
B 109
C 110
D 112

2 Which of these shows the missing piece in the figure?

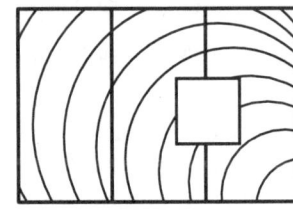

F   H
G   J

3 How many stars would be in the eleventh figure if this pattern continues?

```
★ ★      ★ ★ ★      ★ ★ ★ ★
  ★        ★ ★        ★ ★ ★
★ ★      ★ ★ ★      ★ ★ ★ ★
```

A 25   C 35
B 28   D 42

4 How many dots will form the seventh figure in this pattern?

_____
_____
_____
_____
_____

Answers
SA Ⓐ Ⓑ Ⓒ Ⓓ   1 Ⓐ Ⓑ Ⓒ Ⓓ   2 Ⓕ Ⓖ Ⓗ Ⓙ   3 Ⓐ Ⓑ Ⓒ Ⓓ

65

Using Estimation

Directions: Darken the circle for the correct answer, or write it in the space provided.

TRY THIS — Round numbers when you estimate. For some problems, there are no exact answers. Then you should take your best guess. You can check your answer by using the numbers given in the problem.

Sample A

The closest estimate of the cost of 22 packs of gum is—

1 pack = 47¢

A $0.10
B $1.00
C $10.00
D $100.00

THINK IT THROUGH — The correct answer is C. 22 is rounded to 20, and 47¢ is rounded to 50¢ × 20 = **$10.00**

---

1. During a recent census, the population in Valley View was 6,488. This is an increase of 843 since the last census. What is the best estimate of how many people were counted in the previous census?

   A 5,600   C 7,300
   B 6,800   D 7,500

2. Lila's restaurant bought 28 cases of canned tomatoes. There are 48 cans of tomatoes in each case. What is the best estimate of the total number of cans of tomatoes that the restaurant bought?

   F 600   H 1,500
   G 1,000   J 4,000

3. The distance from Chicago to Atlanta is 708 miles. The distance from Dallas to Atlanta is 822 miles. About how much farther is Dallas from Atlanta than Chicago is from Atlanta?

   A 100 miles   C 800 miles
   B 700 miles   D 1,500 miles

4. Mrs. McMurphy set up trust funds for her 4 children. If she had $22,000 to divide evenly, what is the best estimate of the amount of money in each of the 4 trust funds?

   F $10,000   H $7,000
   G $8,000   J $5,000

5. Mr. Petrovich has 11,200 coins in his collection. He plans to add another 1,600 to his collection this year. What is the best estimate of the number of coins Mr. Petrovich will have at the end of this year?

   A 9,000 coins   C 11,000 coins
   B 10,000 coins   D 13,000 coins

6. Hakeem can throw a football 3 yards. He can throw a baseball 73 yards. What would you have to do to determine how much farther he can throw a baseball than a football?

   _____
   _____
   _____
   _____

Answers

SA Ⓐ Ⓑ Ⓒ Ⓓ   2 Ⓕ Ⓖ Ⓗ Ⓙ   4 Ⓕ Ⓖ Ⓗ Ⓙ
1   Ⓐ Ⓑ Ⓒ Ⓓ   3 Ⓐ Ⓑ Ⓒ Ⓓ   5 Ⓐ Ⓑ Ⓒ Ⓓ

Using Problem-Solving Strategies

Directions: Darken the circle for the correct answer, or write the answer in the space provided.

TRY THIS Study the words in each problem carefully. Think about what each problem is asking, then decide what you have to do to find the answer.

Sample A

Marie works in a bakery. She made 90 fewer bagels on Sunday than she did on Saturday. She made 70 more bagels on Monday than she did on Sunday. If she made 340 bagels on Monday, how many bagels did she make on Saturday?

A 160
B 320
C 360
D 380

THINK IT THROUGH The correct answer is <u>C</u>. Marie made 340 bagels Monday, 270 Sunday, and <u>360</u> on Saturday.

1. Martha is training for a marathon. On Monday she ran 6 miles. On Tuesday she ran 8 miles. On Wednesday she ran 10 miles. On Thursday she ran 12 miles. If this pattern continues, how many miles will she run on Sunday?

   A 14 miles
   B 16 miles
   C 18 miles
   D 20 miles

2. If 1 prism weighs the same as 4 spheres, what do you need to add to Side B to balance the scale?

   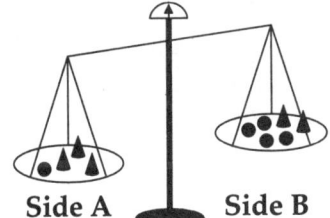
   Side A   Side B

   F 1 prism
   G 1 sphere
   H 3 spheres and 1 prism
   J 2 spheres and 2 prisms

3. Ethan, Kenny, and Lance are brothers. Kenny is not the oldest, and Lance is not the youngest. Ethan is younger than Kenny. Which of these shows the birth order from oldest to youngest?

   A Ethan, Kenny, Lance
   B Kenny, Lance, Ethan
   C Lance, Ethan, Kenny
   D Lance, Kenny, Ethan

4. Elyse took some friends to the movies. The price of a child's ticket was $3.00, and the price of an adult's ticket was $6.00. What do you need to know to find out how much Elyse paid for all of her friends' tickets?

   _____
   _____
   _____
   _____
   _____

Answers
SA Ⓐ Ⓑ Ⓒ Ⓓ   1 Ⓐ Ⓑ Ⓒ Ⓓ   2 Ⓕ Ⓖ Ⓗ Ⓙ   3 Ⓐ Ⓑ Ⓒ Ⓓ

Test

Sample A

What fraction means the same as $4\frac{3}{5}$?

A $\frac{7}{5}$ C $\frac{12}{5}$

B $\frac{23}{5}$ D $\frac{17}{5}$

STOP

For questions 1–42, darken the circle for the correct answer, or write the answer in the space provided.

1. Madelaine has a paperweight collection she wants to give away. How many paperweights would she have to give away if she was going to divide them equally among her 18 cousins with none left over or among her 12 classmates with none left over?

   A 12
   B 18
   C 24
   D 36

2. Attendance at the basketball game was 23,458 last night. This number included 1,000 promotional tickets that were given away. How many paid tickets were used?

   F 22,458
   G 23,358
   H 23,658
   J 24,458

3. In the number 52,658, the 2 means

   A 20
   B 200
   C 2,000
   D 20,000

4. Each square represents 0.05. What decimal number is shown below?

   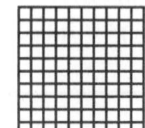 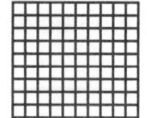 

   F 130.25
   G 13.25
   H 13.025
   J 0.1325

5. What mixed number is shown by the shaded part of the circles?

   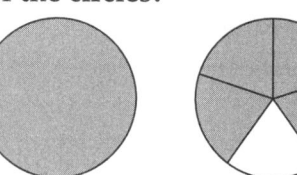

   A $1\frac{5}{6}$
   B $1\frac{1}{5}$
   C $\frac{4}{5}$
   D $1\frac{4}{5}$

6. One week it snowed 6.05 inches. The next week it snowed 6.4 inches. The third week it snowed 6.21 inches. The fourth week it snowed 6.75 inches. How would these amounts of snow be listed in order from least to greatest?

   F 6.05, 6.21, 6.4, 6.75
   G 6.4, 6.75, 6.21, 6.05
   H 6.75, 6.4, 6.05, 6.21
   J 6.21, 6.4, 6.75, 6.05

7. Last year a company sold 3,421,095,804 assorted household gadgets. How is 3,421,095,804 written in words?

   _____
   _____
   _____
   _____
   _____

8   If $x = 4$, $y = 16$, and $z = 5$, what would $x + y + z =$?

   A   29
   B   26
   C   25
   D   21

9   What number is shown here?
    $20{,}000 + 8{,}000 + 400 + 70$

   F   2,847
   G   28,470
   H   28,000,470
   J   208,000,407

10 Michael bought 5 books. He bought 2 art books for $27.99 each. The rest were science-fiction books that cost $6.59 each. Which number sentence could be used to determine how much Michael paid altogether for the books?

   A $(5 - 2) \times \$6.59 = \square$
   B $\$27.99 - \$6.59 = \square$
   C $(2 \times \$27.99) + (3 \times \$6.59) = \square$
   D $(5 - 2) \times (\$27.99 + \$6.59) = \square$

11 Which of the following number sentences is related to $8 \times 7 = \square$?

   F $\square \div 8 = 7$
   G $8 - \square = 7$
   H $8 \div 7 = \square$
   J $8 + 7 = \square$

Julio has 10 letter cards. Use the picture of the cards to answer questions 12 and 13.

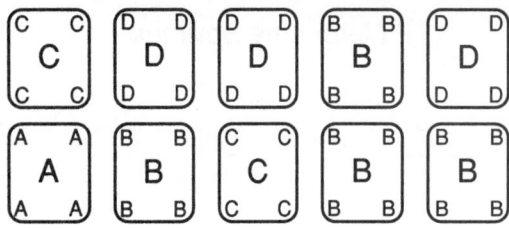

12 If the cards are shuffled and Julio draws 2 cards from the pack at the same time, which of these pairs would he most likely choose?

   A   A, B
   B   B, C
   C   B, D
   D   A, C

13 With his eyes closed, which card will Julio most likely pick and why?

   _____
   _____
   _____
   _____

14 Meili has 4 pairs of white socks, 2 pairs of yellow socks, and 6 pairs of black socks. If she reaches into her sock drawer without looking, what is the probability that she will pick a pair of white socks?

   F $\frac{1}{2}$
   G $\frac{1}{3}$
   H $\frac{1}{4}$
   J $\frac{1}{6}$

The graph below shows the sources of each $100 collected by a local PTA. Use the graph to answer questions 15–17.

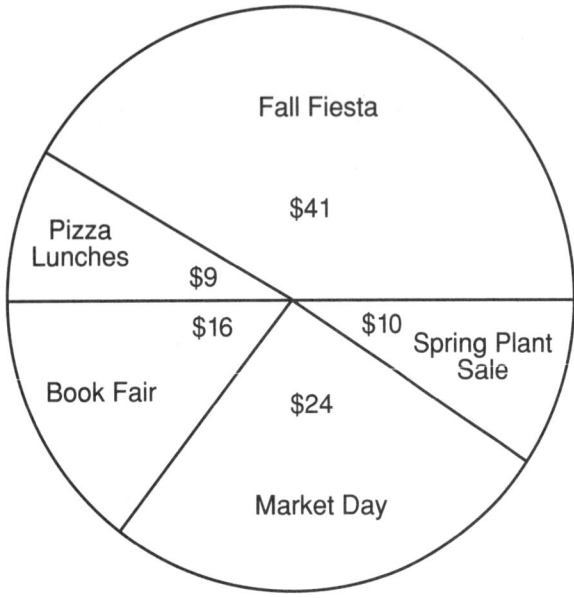

PTA Income Sources

15. Which two sources of income bring in about the same amount of money?

    A Fall Fiesta and Market Day
    B Spring Plant Sale and Pizza Lunches
    C Book Fair and Spring Plant Sale
    D Book Fair and Market Day

16. Which of these income sources is more than twice the Book Fair income?

    F Market Day
    G Fall Fiesta
    H Pizza Lunches
    J Spring Plant Sale

17. How much of each $100 comes from Market Day?

    A $10
    B $16
    C $24
    D $41

The table below shows the rare coins collected by two boys over a four-month period. Use the table to answer questions 18–20.

Rare Coin Collection Record

Reggie	June	July	Aug.	Sept.
Pennies	28	93	86	43
Dimes	12	15	12	18
Len	June	July	Aug.	Sept.
Pennies	14	21	15	14
Dimes	35	24	24	44

18. How many more dimes does Len have than Reggie?

    F 184
    G 80
    H 70
    J 65

19. What was the average number of dimes collected by both boys during the 4 months?

    A 8
    B 46
    C 39
    D 60

20. If the average value of the pennies collected by the two boys was $0.15 per coin, what was the value of their combined penny collections after 4 months?

    _____
    _____
    _____
    _____
    _____
    _____

21 Which line segment names a diameter of the circle shown here?

   F $\overline{AB}$
   G $\overline{XA}$
   H $\overline{AC}$
   J $\overline{XC}$

22 The angle formed by the hands of the clock is—

   A less than 90°
   B exactly 90°
   C exactly 180°
   D more than 90° and less than 180°

23 The graph shows Paul's savings over the last four months. How would the average monthly savings be computed?

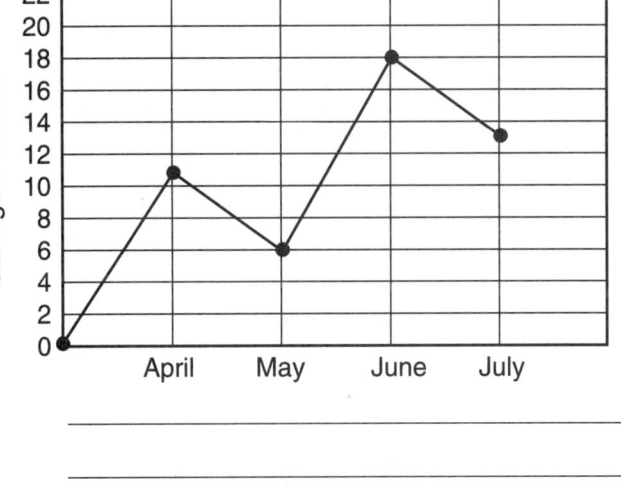

_____
_____
_____
_____

The tally chart below shows points scored by some local teams. Use the chart to answer question 24.

Team	Scores
Eagles	||||	
Lasers	|||| |||| ||||
Falcons	|||| |||| |||| |||
Jets	|||
Bulls	|||| |||| ||

24 Which team scored 6 more points than the Bulls?

   F Eagles
   G Lasers
   H Falcons
   J Jets

25 Manuel is ordering pizza. His choices include thin or thick crust, each with a choice of cheese, sausage, or mushroom toppings. How many different combinations of crusts and toppings are possible?

   A 2
   B 3
   C 5
   D 6

Answers
21 Ⓕ Ⓖ Ⓗ Ⓙ   22 Ⓐ Ⓑ Ⓒ Ⓓ   24 Ⓕ Ⓖ Ⓗ Ⓙ   25 Ⓐ Ⓑ Ⓒ Ⓓ

26 What is the area of the shaded section of this figure?

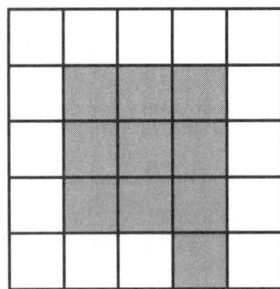

☐ = 1 square unit

- F 10 square units
- G 12 square units
- H 15 square units
- J 16 square units

27 Which figure shows a line of symmetry?

A

B

C

D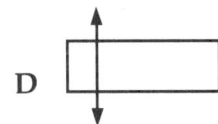

28 Which of the following metric units of measurement is best to use to measure the length of a room?

- F meters
- G liters
- H centimeters
- J kilograms

29 The dress rehearsal began at 2:20 P.M. If it lasted 1 hour and 25 minutes, at what time did the rehearsal end?

- A 6:05 P.M.
- B 5:05 P.M.
- C 3:45 P.M.
- D 2:25 P.M.

30 What are the coordinates of point C?

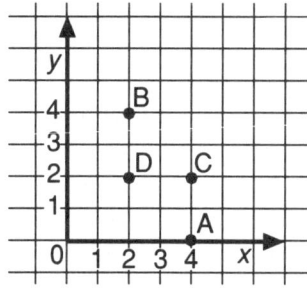

- F (2, 4)
- G (2, 2)
- H (4, 1)
- J (4, 2)

31 The local ice-skating rink is shown here. How would you find the area of the rink?

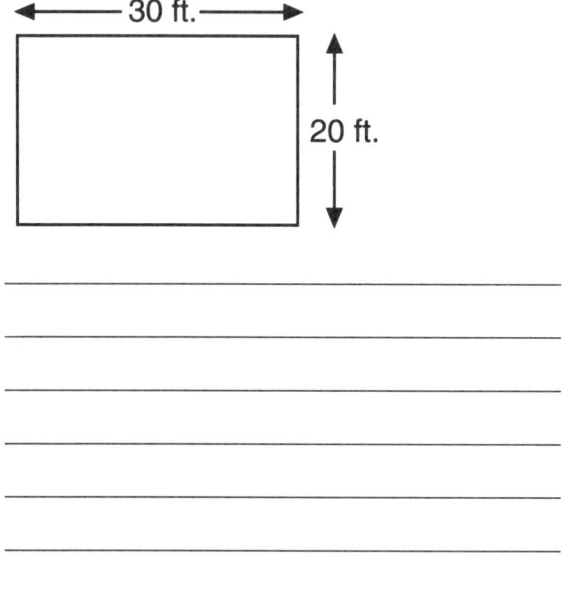

_____
_____
_____
_____
_____
_____

Answers
26 Ⓕ Ⓖ Ⓗ Ⓙ   27 Ⓐ Ⓑ Ⓒ Ⓓ   28 Ⓕ Ⓖ Ⓗ Ⓙ   29 Ⓐ Ⓑ Ⓒ Ⓓ   30 Ⓕ Ⓖ Ⓗ Ⓙ

32 If the pattern shown here continues, how many dots would there be in the seventh figure in the pattern?

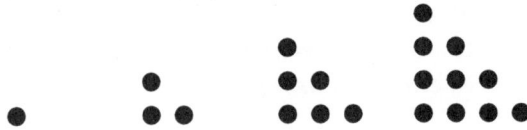

- A 20
- B 28
- C 30
- D 32

33 Use your inch ruler and the map to help you answer the question. What is the actual distance between the two bridges?

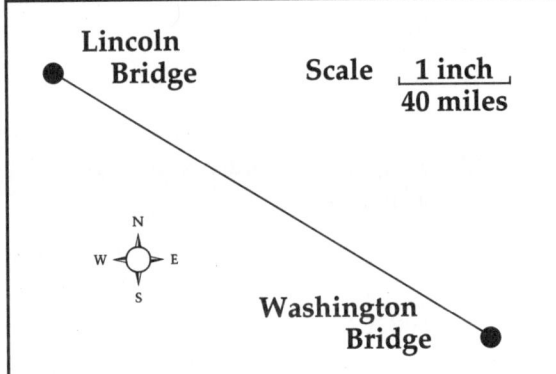

- F 120 miles
- G 110 miles
- H 100 miles
- J   90 miles

34 Jon has played soccer for 14 years, the longest of his 5 friends. Charles has played soccer for only 9 years, fewer years than his friends. What is the best estimate of the total number of years all 6 friends have played soccer?

- A 209 years
- B 125 years
- C 90 years
- D 70 years

35 A special machine multiplies any number entered into it by a secret number. The table shows how numbers are changed. Which number is missing from the table?

Original number	5	9	11
New number	25	45	

- F 75
- G 65
- H 60
- J 55

36 Chris is older than Sam. Ralph is older than Sam, but younger than Chris. Sam is younger than Ben. Chris is not the oldest. List the boys in order from youngest to oldest.

_____

_____

_____

Answers
32 Ⓐ Ⓑ Ⓒ Ⓓ   33 Ⓕ Ⓖ Ⓗ Ⓙ   34 Ⓐ Ⓑ Ⓒ Ⓓ   35 Ⓕ Ⓖ Ⓗ Ⓙ

37 To raise funds for a special project, the Girls' Athletic Association ordered 450 flowers from a nursery to sell at school. The nursery charged $0.35 each for the daisies and $0.45 each for the carnations. If the sales tax is 7.25%, what other information is needed to find the total cost of the flowers?

  A the colors of the flowers
  B how many flowers each member is required to sell
  C the total number of members in the Girls' Athletic Association
  D how many of each kind of flower was ordered

38 At the supermarket yesterday, Lucas bought 3 magazines at $2.85 each. About how much money did he spend altogether?

  F $10.50
  G $9.00
  H $7.00
  J $6.50

39 Carl has 36 fish in one aquarium and 52 fish in another aquarium. How many fish should he move from the second aquarium in order to have the same number of fish in both aquariums?

  A 24
  B 16
  C 12
  D 8

40 There were four cross-country team members running in an event. Robin finished after Earl. Nick finished after Robin. Neal finished ahead of Robin but after Earl. Which of the following shows the order in which the runners finished the event from first to last?

  F Earl, Neal, Robin, Nick
  G Neal, Earl, Robin, Nick
  H Robin, Earl, Nick, Neal
  J Nick, Robin, Neal, Earl

41 Maria went to the zoo with friends from school on Saturday. What do you *not* need to know to find out how much money Maria had left when she got home?

  A how much money Maria spent on snacks
  B how much money Maria's ticket to the zoo cost
  C how much money Maria spent on souvenirs
  D how long Maria stayed at the zoo

42 In 1790, the population of the United States was 3,929,000. What other information do you need to know to find how much the population has increased since then?

___

Answers
37 Ⓐ Ⓑ Ⓒ Ⓓ   38 Ⓕ Ⓖ Ⓗ Ⓙ   39 Ⓐ Ⓑ Ⓒ Ⓓ   40 Ⓕ Ⓖ Ⓗ Ⓙ   41 Ⓐ Ⓑ Ⓒ Ⓓ

Math Procedures Using Computation

Directions: Darken the circle for the correct answer, or write the answer in the space provided. Darken the circle for *NH, Not Here,* if the correct answer is not given.

TRY THIS — Work the problem on scratch paper. Then check your answer before comparing it to the answer choices where given. Check the answer to a division problem by multiplying.

Sample A

$526 \times 37 =$

A 19,462
B 19,252
C 18,264
D 563
E NH

THINK IT THROUGH — The correct answer is A. When 526 is multiplied by 37, the answer is 19,462.

---

1. $4563 \div 9 =$

A 590 R4
B 548
C 507
D 57
E NH

2. $0.6 \times 0.9 =$

F 5.4
G 0.54
H 0.054
J 0.0054
K NH

3. $\frac{1}{4} + \frac{1}{3}$

A $\frac{14}{32}$
B $\frac{1}{2}$
C $\frac{7}{12}$
D $\frac{8}{12}$
E NH

4. $0.762 - 0.471 =$

F 1.233
G 0.309
H 0.299
J 0.281
K NH

5. $7\frac{2}{3}$
   $+ 10\frac{1}{4}$

A $17\frac{3}{7}$
B $17\frac{10}{12}$
C $17\frac{11}{12}$
D $18\frac{1}{12}$
E NH

6. $\frac{5}{8} \times \frac{2}{7} =$

_____
_____
_____
_____

Answers

SA Ⓐ Ⓑ Ⓒ Ⓓ Ⓔ
1   Ⓐ Ⓑ Ⓒ Ⓓ Ⓔ
2   Ⓕ Ⓖ Ⓗ Ⓙ Ⓚ
3   Ⓐ Ⓑ Ⓒ Ⓓ Ⓔ
4   Ⓕ Ⓖ Ⓗ Ⓙ Ⓚ
5   Ⓐ Ⓑ Ⓒ Ⓓ Ⓔ

Using Computation in Context

Directions: Darken the circle for the correct answer, or write the answer in the space provided. Darken the circle for NH, Not Here, if the correct answer is not given.

> **TRY THIS** Read the word problem carefully. Then set up the word problem as a computation problem. Work the problem on scratch paper and compare the answer with the answer choices given.

Sample A

Sonia bought 80 plants from her garden supplier.

If the plants cost $22.75 each, what was the total cost of the plants before tax was added?

A $1,760
B $1,800
C $1,820
D $1,860
E NH

> **THINK IT THROUGH** The correct answer is C. To find the total cost multiply 80 x 22.75. The total cost is $1,820.

1. Miguel is buying a camera for $58.59. What is this amount rounded to the nearest dollar?

   A $60.00
   B $59.00
   C $88.60
   D $58.00
   E NH

2. At an arts-and-crafts fair, $\frac{1}{3}$ of the vendors are selling wooden handicrafts and $\frac{1}{6}$ are selling paintings.

   How many of the vendors at the arts-and-crafts fair are selling either wooden handicrafts or paintings?

   F $\frac{2}{9}$
   G $\frac{1}{3}$
   H $\frac{1}{2}$
   J $\frac{2}{3}$
   K NH

3. Kyle collects models of all kinds. He has 14 model trucks, 12 model airplanes, and 23 model cars. How many models does Kyle have altogether?

   A 28
   B 31
   C 37
   D 49
   E NH

4. Mr. Jackson bought 64 ounces of orange juice for his family. If each of the 8 family members received 8 ounces of juice, what percent of the total did each person receive?

   _____
   _____
   _____
   _____

Answers
SA Ⓐ Ⓑ Ⓒ Ⓓ Ⓔ   1 Ⓐ Ⓑ Ⓒ Ⓓ Ⓔ   2 Ⓕ Ⓖ Ⓗ Ⓙ Ⓚ   3 Ⓐ Ⓑ Ⓒ Ⓓ Ⓔ

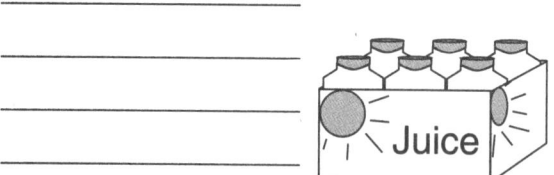

Test

Sample A

$\frac{7}{9} \times \frac{3}{5} =$

A $\frac{10}{45}$
B $\frac{7}{15}$
C $\frac{27}{35}$
D $\frac{10}{14}$
E NH

Sample B

$344 \div 7 =$

F 39
G 49 R1
H 49RS
J 50
K NH

Directions: Darken the circle for the correct answer. Darken the circle for NH, Not Here, if the correct answer is not given. If no choices are given, write in the answer.

1. $0.4 \times 0.8 =$

A 0.0032
B 0.032
C 0.32
D 3.2
E NH

2. $\frac{3}{8} + \frac{6}{24}$

F $\frac{9}{32}$
G $\frac{1}{2}$
H $\frac{5}{8}$
J $\frac{3}{4}$
K NH

3. $0.7 \times 0.8 =$

A 0.056
B 0.506
C 0.56
D 5.6
E NH

4. Rosa went on a fishing trip last weekend. On Saturday she caught 11 fish, and on Sunday she caught 16 fish.

   How many fish did she catch altogether?

F 37
G 27
H 19
J 5
K NH

5. $92 \times 54 =$

A 5,298
B 5,008
C 4,978
D 4,968
E NH

6. $1.908 - 0.564 =$

F 1.344
G 1.244
H 1.094
J 0.986
K NH

7. $14.357 - 11.269 =$

A 3.080
B 3.112
C 3.808
D 3.880
E NH

8. What must you do first, before solving this problem?

   $\frac{1}{4} - \frac{1}{6}$

   _____
   _____
   _____
   _____
   _____
   _____

Answers

SA Ⓐ Ⓑ Ⓒ Ⓓ Ⓔ
SB Ⓕ Ⓖ Ⓗ Ⓙ Ⓚ
1 Ⓐ Ⓑ Ⓒ Ⓓ Ⓔ
2 Ⓕ Ⓖ Ⓗ Ⓙ Ⓚ
3 Ⓐ Ⓑ Ⓒ Ⓓ Ⓔ
4 Ⓕ Ⓖ Ⓗ Ⓙ Ⓚ
5 Ⓐ Ⓑ Ⓒ Ⓓ Ⓔ
6 Ⓕ Ⓖ Ⓗ Ⓙ Ⓚ
7 Ⓐ Ⓑ Ⓒ Ⓓ Ⓔ

9. Last year a store sold 1,657 radios. This year the store sold 423 radios.

   How many radios did they sell in the two years altogether?

   F 2,090
   G 2,190
   H 2,881
   J 5,887
   K NH

10. Donna set a goal to swim 32 laps in the pool without stopping. After 24 laps she stopped to rest.

    What percent of her goal did Donna complete?

    A 125%
    B 75%
    C 60%
    D 25%
    E NH

11. The Atlantic Ocean covers approximately 41,000,000 square miles.

    What is that number rounded to the nearest million?

    41,000,000

    _____
    _____
    _____
    _____

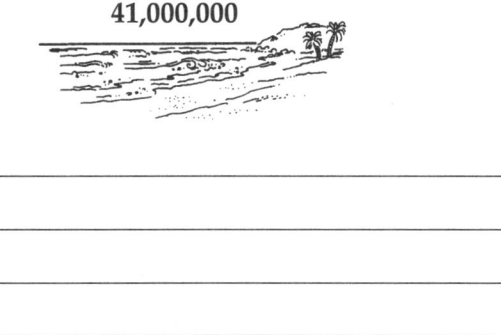

12. Every day Jenny and Lori ride their bicycles $1\frac{1}{2}$ kilometers to school. They ride $\frac{3}{4}$ kilometer to the park.

    $1\frac{1}{2}$ km

    How much farther is their ride to school than to the park?

    F $\frac{1}{8}$ kilometer
    G $\frac{1}{6}$ kilometer
    H $\frac{3}{4}$ kilometer
    J $\frac{4}{5}$ kilometer
    K NH

    $\frac{3}{4}$ km

13. There are 300 summer campers at Camp Willow.

    If $\frac{3}{5}$ of the campers are boys, how many boys are there at Camp Willow?

    A 180
    B 150
    C 120
    D 100
    E NH

Answers

9 F G H J K
10 A B C D E
12 F G H J K
13 A B C D E

UNIT SEVEN
Listening

Understanding Word Meanings

Directions: Darken the circle for the word or words that best complete the sentence you hear.

TRY THIS — Listen carefully to the sentence. Then look at the answer choices. Decide which words you know are wrong. Then look at the remaining words to make your choice.

Sample A
- A clean
- B paint
- C decorate
- D simplify

THINK IT THROUGH — The correct answer is C.

1
- A considered
- B announced
- C reported
- D called

2
- F rough
- G dry
- H red
- J wet

3
- A a choice
- B a mistake
- C a promise
- D an agreement

4
- F a melody
- G a strike
- H a memory
- J an effect

5
- A a game
- B an event
- C an insult
- D a misunderstanding

6
- F truthful
- G excellent
- H frail
- J believable

7
- A an appointment
- B a suggestion
- C a result
- D an argument

8
- F essential
- G worthless
- H severe
- J eternal

9
- A reward
- B chapter
- C chore
- D book

10
- F noticeable
- G distant
- H close
- J unseen

Answers
SA Ⓐ Ⓑ Ⓒ Ⓓ
1   Ⓐ Ⓑ Ⓒ Ⓓ
2   Ⓕ Ⓖ Ⓗ Ⓙ
3   Ⓐ Ⓑ Ⓒ Ⓓ
4   Ⓕ Ⓖ Ⓗ Ⓙ
5   Ⓐ Ⓑ Ⓒ Ⓓ
6   Ⓕ Ⓖ Ⓗ Ⓙ
7   Ⓐ Ⓑ Ⓒ Ⓓ
8   Ⓕ Ⓖ Ⓗ Ⓙ
9   Ⓐ Ⓑ Ⓒ Ⓓ
10 Ⓕ Ⓖ Ⓗ Ⓙ

Building Listening Skills

Directions: Darken the circle for the word or words that best answer the question.

TRY THIS — Form a picture of the story in your mind. Listen carefully for details given in the story.

Sample A

A long
B braided
C dyed
D short

THINK IT THROUGH — The correct answer is A. Denise probably smiled because her hair in the back was long, which is what she requested.

1.
   A are cold–blooded
   B have gills
   C are small killer whales
   D have teeth

2.
   F maintain their body temperature
   G come to the surface
   H swim toward warm water
   J cannot breathe

3.
   A fish
   B mammals
   C whales
   D reptiles

4.
   F breathe oxygen
   G hide from whales
   H communicate with other dolphins
   J get warm

5.
   A Mississippi
   B Arkansas
   C Ohio
   D Texas

6.
   F to play cards
   G to hold a swap meet
   H to exchange news
   J to get in line to buy items from the store

7.
   A a writer
   B a store clerk
   C a politician
   D a reporter

8.
   F conserve resources
   G keep the house warmer
   H use other resources more frequently
   J stop using natural resources

9.
   A wash small loads of dishes
   B avoid washing clothes in hot water
   C leave lights on all day
   D set the thermostat higher in winter

10.
    F It should be turned down.
    G It should be turned off.
    H It should be turned up.
    J It should be set as low as possible.

Answers

SA Ⓐ Ⓑ Ⓒ Ⓓ
1 Ⓐ Ⓑ Ⓒ Ⓓ
2 Ⓕ Ⓖ Ⓗ Ⓙ
3 Ⓐ Ⓑ Ⓒ Ⓓ
4 Ⓕ Ⓖ Ⓗ Ⓙ
5 Ⓐ Ⓑ Ⓒ Ⓓ
6 Ⓕ Ⓖ Ⓗ Ⓙ
7 Ⓐ Ⓑ Ⓒ Ⓓ
8 Ⓕ Ⓖ Ⓗ Ⓙ
9 Ⓐ Ⓑ Ⓒ Ⓓ
10 Ⓕ Ⓖ Ⓗ Ⓙ

Test

Sample A
- A drab
- B rich
- C attractive
- D simple

🛑

For questions 1–13, darken the circle for the word or words that best complete the sentence you hear.

1.
- A endless
- B limited
- C little
- D simple

2.
- F reschedule
- G assign
- H make
- J cancel

3.
- A separate
- B include
- C unite
- D illustrate

4.
- F fruit
- G vegetables
- H grass
- J leaves

5.
- A canceled
- B opened
- C delayed
- D finished

6.
- F agreement
- G approval
- H joy
- J disagreement

7.
- A soak
- B tremble
- C sneeze
- D groan

8.
- F small
- G alone
- H energetic
- J sad

9.
- A deliver it
- B accept it
- C refuse it
- D crave it

10.
- F cloth
- G fable
- H dress
- J yarn

11.
- A a problem
- B a solution
- C an election
- D an article

12.
- F lost
- G left out
- H included
- J repeated

13.
- A order
- B calendar
- C plan
- D advertisement

Answers
- SA Ⓐ Ⓑ Ⓒ Ⓓ
- 1 Ⓐ Ⓑ Ⓒ Ⓓ
- 2 Ⓕ Ⓖ Ⓗ Ⓙ
- 3 Ⓐ Ⓑ Ⓒ Ⓓ
- 4 Ⓕ Ⓖ Ⓗ Ⓙ
- 5 Ⓐ Ⓑ Ⓒ Ⓓ
- 6 Ⓕ Ⓖ Ⓗ Ⓙ
- 7 Ⓐ Ⓑ Ⓒ Ⓓ
- 8 Ⓕ Ⓖ Ⓗ Ⓙ
- 9 Ⓐ Ⓑ Ⓒ Ⓓ
- 10 Ⓕ Ⓖ Ⓗ Ⓙ
- 11 Ⓐ Ⓑ Ⓒ Ⓓ
- 12 Ⓕ Ⓖ Ⓗ Ⓙ
- 13 Ⓐ Ⓑ Ⓒ Ⓓ

Sample B

A flower   C tree
B food   D fish

For questions 14–26, listen to the story. Then darken the circle for the word or words that best answer the question.

14 F directions
    G young apple trees
    H barrels of apples
    J books of songs

15 A dog
    B wolf
    C buffalo
    D coyote

16 F a fictional character
    G a settler
    H a helpful person
    J a musician

17 A Virginia
    B Ohio
    C Massachusetts
    D the West

18 F age 18
    G age 35
    H age 45
    J age 48

19 A work very hard
    B have long careers
    C have easy lives
    D rarely practice

20 F make money
    G practice every day
    H teach other dancers
    J learn to act

21 A at five years of age
    B at seventeen or eighteen years of age
    C when they are adults
    D at seven years of age

22 F seventeen years old
    G eight years old
    H twelve years
    J five years old

23 A wear a hat
    B wear eye–safety gear
    C wear good sunglasses
    D stay in the shade

24 F an encyclopedia
    G a pharmacy
    H a science magazine
    J a newspaper

25 A use a dim light
    B wear sunglasses
    C wear eye-safety gear
    D use plenty of light

26 F prevent eyestrain
    G get regular eye exams
    H wear eye-safety gear
    J avoid close work

Answers

SB Ⓐ Ⓑ Ⓒ Ⓓ   16 Ⓕ Ⓖ Ⓗ Ⓙ   19 Ⓐ Ⓑ Ⓒ Ⓓ   22 Ⓕ Ⓖ Ⓗ Ⓙ   25 Ⓐ Ⓑ Ⓒ Ⓓ
14 Ⓕ Ⓖ Ⓗ Ⓙ   17 Ⓐ Ⓑ Ⓒ Ⓓ   20 Ⓕ Ⓖ Ⓗ Ⓙ   23 Ⓐ Ⓑ Ⓒ Ⓓ   26 Ⓕ Ⓖ Ⓗ Ⓙ
15 Ⓐ Ⓑ Ⓒ Ⓓ   18 Ⓕ Ⓖ Ⓗ Ⓙ   21 Ⓐ Ⓑ Ⓒ Ⓓ   24 Ⓕ Ⓖ Ⓗ Ⓙ

UNIT EIGHT
Language

Prewriting, Composing, and Editing

Directions: Read each sentence carefully. Then darken the circle for the correct answer to each question, or write the answer in the space provided.

TRY THIS Pretend that you are writing each sentence. Use the rules you have learned for capitalization, punctuation, word usage, and sentence structure to choose the correct answer.

Delivering Mail by Pony Express

In his social studies class, Guido learned about the pony express, a mail delivery service in the Old West. He wanted to learn more details about the history of this mail service. Guido decided to use this as the subject of his research paper for social studies class.

Sample A

Guido is reading the book *The First Overland Mail* to help him with his research. Where should he look to find the name of the author of the book?

A the bibliography

B the title page

C the index

D the table of contents

THINK IT THROUGH The correct answer is <u>B</u>. The author's name is found on the <u>title page</u>

Traveling by Bicycle

Alyson wants to organize a bicycle tour for her scouting group. She is interested in traveling along one of the bicycle paths in the forest preserves located in her county. Alyson decides to write a letter to obtain information about bicycling in the county forest preserves.

Dear County Forest Preserve Director,
   I am writing to ask you to send me a map of bicycle paths in our county forest preserves. I am organizing a bicycle tour for my scouting group. When you can send it. I need to make arrangements as soon as possible.

1 Which of these is <u>not</u> a complete sentence?

A I am writing to ask you to send me a map of bicycle paths in our county forest preserves.

B I am organizing a bicycle tour for my scouting group.

C When you can send it.

D I need to make arrangements as soon as possible.

Answers
SA Ⓐ Ⓑ Ⓒ Ⓓ   1 Ⓐ Ⓑ Ⓒ Ⓓ

83

Guido used the dictionary to look up some words for his report.

2   Which definition of the word *switch* is used in the following sentence?

   The pony express rider would *switch* to a fresh horse at each relay station.

   F   beat with a stick

   G   move suddenly

   H   change

   J   break an electrical circuit

3   The "a" in *dangerous* sounds most like the vowel sound in—

   A   travel

   B   locate

   C   barometer

   D   necklace

Guido used the information he found on the pony express to make a concept web. Use the concept web to answer questions 4 and 5.

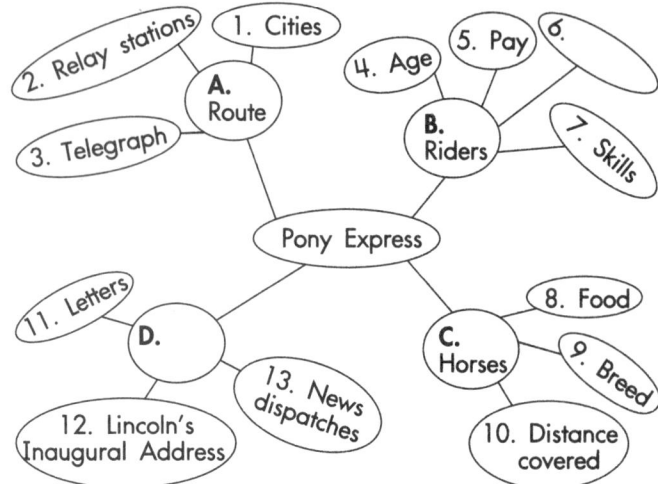

4   Which of these belongs in circle D?

   F   Mail

   G   Stagecoaches

   H   Mining camps

   J   Swing stations

5   Which of these belongs in number 6 next to circle B?

   A   St. Joseph, Missouri

   B   Weight

   C   Mustangs

   D $5 a half-ounce

Here is a rough draft of the first part of Guido's paper. Read the rough draft carefully. Then answer questions 6–10.

Delivering Mail by Pony Express

The gold rush in California in the 1840s and 1850s brought thousands of
(1)

people to the West. Most of them were seeking gold. They had left family
(2) (3)

members in the eastern part of the United States. Families and friends in the
(4)

East waited to hear from their loved ones who had moved west.

In 1860, the fastest method of delivering mail was by stagecoach.
(5)

Unfortunately, this delivery system took 25 days in some cases, the wait
(6)

for mail was even longer. This was especially true in mining camps where
(7)

letters took three to four months to be delivered.

In 1860, a businessman named William Hepburn Russell devised a plan for
(8)

a faster mail delivery system. His mail service would take just ten days. The
(9) (10)

Civil War lasted for four years. Russell spent $100,000 on the pony express
(11)

with the hope of making a fortune. He built 190 stations on the pony express
(12)

trail. It extended and stretched for 1,800 miles through the western frontier.
(13)

The eastern terminal was in St. Joseph, Missouri, and the western terminal
(14)

was in Sacramento, California.

6 Which is a run-on sentence?

- F 5
- G 6
- H 7
- J 8

7 Which of the following sentences could be added after sentence 7?

- A St. Joseph, Missouri, was the western end of the United States railroad service.
- B When the relay stationkeeper heard hoof beats, he would get a fresh horse ready.
- C Therefore, miners hungered for a faster mail delivery service.
- D As a result of this, few young men applied for the job as a pony express rider.

8 How can sentences 2 and 3 best be combined?

- F Most of them were seeking gold and had left behind family members in the eastern United States.
- G They had left family members in the eastern part of the United States most whom were seeking gold.
- H Most of them were seeking gold and family members in the eastern part of the United States.
- J They were seeking gold in the eastern part of the United States who had left behind family members.

9 What is the most colorful way to write sentence 4?

- A Families and friends back East anxiously awaited word from their loved ones who had traveled west.
- B Families and friends in the East waited to receive letters from their loved ones who had moved west.
- C Families and friends waited for long periods of time to receive letters from their loved ones in the West.
- D As it is written.

10 Which sentence does not belong in Guido's report and why?

_____
_____
_____
_____
_____

Answers

6 Ⓕ Ⓖ Ⓗ Ⓙ   7 Ⓐ Ⓑ Ⓒ Ⓓ   8 Ⓕ Ⓖ Ⓗ Ⓙ   9 Ⓐ Ⓑ Ⓒ Ⓓ

Here is the next part of Guido's rough draft for his research paper. This part has certain words and phrases underlined. Read the draft carefully. Then answer questions 11–16.

William Hepburn Russell bought 500 horses for his new business. The
(15) (16)

horses were wild mustangs that had been rounded up on the plains. Each
(17)

horse were broken by a cowboy. Russell hired 80 men—usually
(18)

teen-agers—as pony express riders. A riders' job as a mail carrier on
(19)

the pony express trail was dangerous. These young men carried the mail
(20)

through deserts, over mountains, through rain, snow, extreme heat, and

unfriendly Native American territory. They risked their lives daily. As one
(21) (22)

rider explained "It is dangerous work, but I know it's an important service."

When President Abraham Lincoln gave his first speech to Congress, a copy
(23)

of it was carried to Sacramento by the pony express.

The pony express riders are carrying the mail for 75 miles a workday.
(24)

They stopped at relay stations every 5 to 10 miles to switch horses. A
(25) (26)

rider's workday ended at a swing, or home station, where hed eat and sleep

between runs. Another rider at the station would take the mail and
(27)

continue the run. The pony express rider received from $100 to $150 a
(28)

month for this dangerous work.

11 In sentence 16, had been rounded up is best written—

F will be rounded up
G have been rounded up
H are going to be rounded up
J As it is written.

12 In sentence 17, were broken is best written—

A has broken
B broken
C was broken
D As it is written.

13 In sentence 19, A riders' job is best written—

F A riders jobs
G A rider's job
H A riders job
J As it is written.

14 In sentence 22, explained "It is dangerous is best written—

A explained, "It is dangerous
B explained "It, is dangerous
C explained, "it is dangerous
D As it is written.

15 In sentence 24, riders are carrying is best written—

F rider's are carrying
G riders are known to carry
H riders carried
J As it is written.

16 In sentence 26, where hed eat and sleep is best written—

A where he'd eat and sleep
B where he'ld eat and sleep
C where hew'd eat and sleep
D As it is written.

Answers
11 Ⓕ Ⓖ Ⓗ Ⓙ   13 Ⓕ Ⓖ Ⓗ Ⓙ   15 Ⓕ Ⓖ Ⓗ Ⓙ
12 Ⓐ Ⓑ Ⓒ Ⓓ   14 Ⓐ Ⓑ Ⓒ Ⓓ   16 Ⓐ Ⓑ Ⓒ Ⓓ

Identifying Misspelled Words

Directions: Read each sentence carefully. If one of the words is misspelled, darken the circle for that word. If all the words are spelled correctly, darken the circle for *No mistake*.

> **TRY THIS** Read each sentence carefully. If you are not sure of an answer, first decide which answer choices are spelled correctly. Then see if you can recognize the misspelled word from your reading experience.

Sample A

Aunt Jane <u>remarked</u> that Tommy had <u>groan</u> three <u>inches</u>. <u>No mistake</u>
        A   B   C   D

> **THINK IT THROUGH** The correct choice is **B**. When you increase in size, the word is spelled grown. Groan is the sound you might make when you are in pain.

---

1. Bernard <u>kickt</u> the <u>soccer</u> ball <u>high</u> in the air. <u>No mistake</u>
        A   B   C   D

2. She <u>asked</u> us to please <u>reafrain</u> from <u>walking</u> on the grass. <u>No mistake</u>
   F   G   H   J

3. He <u>appealled</u> the <u>jury's</u> <u>decision</u> on the <u>case</u>. No mistake
   A   B   C   D

4. The crowd <u>reacted</u> <u>positively</u> to the speaker's <u>statements</u>. <u>No mistake</u>
      F   G   H   J

5. The <u>peel</u> of the <u>church</u> bells rang <u>throughout</u> the valley. <u>No mistake</u>
    A   B   C   D

6. Being on top of a <u>mountain</u> can give you the <u>lonelyest</u> <u>feeling</u>. <u>No mistake</u>
               F   G   H   J

7. We had a long <u>converseation</u> on <u>Thursday</u> <u>evening</u>. <u>No mistake</u>
            A   B   C   D

8. Guillermo was <u>agonizing</u> over his <u>difficult</u> <u>decision</u>. <u>No mistake</u>
      F   G   H   J

Answers

SA Ⓐ Ⓑ Ⓒ Ⓓ   3 Ⓐ Ⓑ Ⓒ Ⓓ   6 Ⓕ Ⓖ Ⓗ Ⓙ
1 Ⓐ Ⓑ Ⓒ Ⓓ   4 Ⓕ Ⓖ Ⓗ Ⓙ   7 Ⓐ Ⓑ Ⓒ Ⓓ
2 Ⓕ Ⓖ Ⓗ Ⓙ   5 Ⓐ Ⓑ Ⓒ Ⓓ   8 Ⓕ Ⓖ Ⓗ Ⓙ

Sample B

Many of the Native Americans on the (1) Great Plains had migrated from the eastern woodlands because of increasing populations and the arrival of the Europeans. Many of (2) these Native Americans depended upon the

How is sentence 2 best written?

A Many of these Native Americans depended upon the buffalo for food clothing shelter and even fuel.

B Many of these Native Americans depended upon the buffalo for food, clothing, shelter, and even fuel.

C Many of these Native Americans depended upon the buffalo for: food, clothing, shelter, and even fuel.

D As it is written.

Keiko is reading the book *Everglades National Park*. Study the Table of Contents from that book. Then answer questions 1 and 2.

Table of Contents

Chapter	Page
1 A Swamp Walk	8
2 Alligator Homes	12
3 Species of Snakes	15
4 Biking and Hiking	21
5 Camping and Other Facilities	30

1 Which chapter should Keiko read to find information about recreational activities in the Everglades?

    A Chapter 1   C Chapter 3

    B Chapter 2   D Chapter 4

2 Which chapter should Keiko read to learn about the habitat of alligators?

_____

_____

_____

Keiko's Trip

Keiko is on a trip to the Florida Everglades with her family. Keiko is excited because the Everglades is such an unusual place to visit. She decides to write a letter to her friend Erin about the Everglades.

3 Keiko cannot remember the correct way to write a friendly letter. In which reference source could she find an example of one?

    F an almanac

    G a science textbook

    H an atlas

    J an English textbook

4 Why is Keiko writing a letter?

    A to ask Erin for further information about the Everglades

    B to tell Erin about her trip to the Everglades

    C to invite Erin on a trip to the Everglades

    D to ask Erin to send her a map of the Everglades

Answers

SB Ⓐ Ⓑ Ⓒ Ⓓ   1 Ⓐ Ⓑ Ⓒ Ⓓ   3 Ⓕ Ⓖ Ⓗ Ⓙ   4 Ⓐ Ⓑ Ⓒ Ⓓ

Here is a rough draft of the first part of Keiko's letter. Read the rough draft carefully. Then answer questions 5–8.

> April 27, 1998
>
> Dear Erin,
>
> My family and me a week ago arrived at Everglades National Park. I am
> (1)   (2)
>
> learning about the wildlife in the Everglades my family and I spend our
>
> days canoeing along marked waterways called trails.
>
> So far we have followed the easiest trails in the park. The West Lake
> (3)   (4)
>
> Trail is a seven-hour trip. Another trip is along the Bear Lake Trail. It
>   (5)   (6)
>
> is a twelve-mile paddle. Next year we plan to go backpacking in the Ozarks.
>   (7)
>
> It was on this trip I saw my first alligator! I thought I would be afraid of
> (8)   (9)
>
> alligators, but they are usually sunning themselves along the banks.

5 Which sentence does not belong in Keiko's letter?

F 4   H 7
G 6   J 9

6 Which of the following sentences could be added after sentence 1?

A I have become an expert at paddling a canoe.
B We are camping in our trailer at Long Pine Campground.
C We had shrimp for dinner last night.
D Dad tripped over the canoe and fell into the lake!

7 What is the best way to write sentence 1?

F My family and I arrived at Everglades National Park a week ago.
G A week ago I and my family arrived at Everglades National Park.
H Me and my family arrived a week ago at Everglades National Park.
J As it is written.

8 Which sentence is a run-on and how would you correct it?

_____
_____
_____

Answers
5 Ⓕ Ⓖ Ⓗ Ⓙ   6 Ⓐ Ⓑ Ⓒ Ⓓ   7 Ⓕ Ⓖ Ⓗ Ⓙ

Here is the next part of Keiko's rough draft of her letter. This part has certain words and phrases underlined. Read the rough draft carefully. Then answer questions 9–14.

I've <u>also seen</u> hundreds of different species of birds. My <u>favorite bird are</u>
   (10)   (11)

<u>the white ibis</u>. This bird has a long beak that curves down. It is all white
      (12)   (13)

except for the ends of its wings which are tipped with black.

Another species of bird that is abundant in Everglades National Park is
   (14)

the heron. There are many kinds of herons that live in the park.
      (15)

Yesterday when we were canoeing in Bear Lake, my father <u>whispered</u>
  (16)

"<u>Look, bald</u> eagles. Eagles are so graceful. What a large wingspan <u>they have</u>!"
      (17)   (18)

Tomorrow <u>we went</u> on a bike hike. We expect to see several kinds of
   (19)   (20)

trees along the bike path. One tree I am looking forward to seeing is the
                    (21)

gumbo limbo tree. This unusual tree has adapted to living in hurricane
   (22)

country. If it is blown over, any part of it that touches the ground sends out
   (23)

roots and goes on growing!

                                                     <u>Your best friend</u>

                                                     Keiko

9 In sentence 10, <u>I've also seen</u> is best written—

A You've also seen

B Iv'e also seen

C Ih've also seen

D As it is written.

10 In sentence 11, <u>favorite bird are the white ibis</u> is best written—

F favorite bird has been the white ibis

G favorite bird will be the white ibis

H favorite bird is the white ibis

J As it is written.

11 In sentence 16, <u>whispered "Look, bald</u> is best written—

A whispered, "Look, bald

B whispered "look, bald

C Whispered Look, bald

D As it is written.

12 In sentence 18, <u>they have!"</u> is best written—

F they have,"

G they have!

H they have.

J As it is written.

13 In sentence 19, <u>we went</u> is best written—

A we weren't

B we was

C we are going

D As it is written.

14 At the end of Keiko's letter, <u>Your best friend</u> is best written—

F your best friend

G Your Best Friend,

H Your best friend,

J As it is written.

Answers

9 Ⓐ Ⓑ Ⓒ Ⓓ   11 Ⓐ Ⓑ Ⓒ Ⓓ   13 Ⓐ Ⓑ Ⓒ Ⓓ
10 Ⓕ Ⓖ Ⓗ Ⓙ   12 Ⓕ Ⓖ Ⓗ Ⓙ   14 Ⓕ Ⓖ Ⓗ Ⓙ

For questions 15–26, read each sentence carefully. If one of the words is misspelled, darken the circle for that word. If all of the words are spelled correctly, darken the circle for *No mistake*.

15 Ralph received a <u>certificate</u> when he <u>finished</u> <u>lifeguard</u> <u>training</u>. <u>No mistake</u>
                              A   B   C   D

16 Marge <u>translatet</u> several journal <u>articles</u> for the <u>university</u>. <u>No mistake</u>
                  F   G   H   J

17 Chameleons use <u>camouflage</u> to <u>avoid</u> becoming the <u>pray</u> of other animals. <u>No mistake</u>
                                A   B   C   D

18 Rosa <u>receives</u> an <u>allowance</u> of ten dollars <u>every</u> week. <u>No mistake</u>
                 F   G   H   J

19 Tom hit two <u>consecutive</u> <u>fowl</u> balls in the second <u>inning</u>. <u>No mistake</u>
                          A   B   C   D

20 Michael has <u>always</u> had a very <u>vivid</u> <u>imagineation</u>. <u>No mistake</u>
                          F   G   H   J

21 I hope to <u>reagain</u> <u>complete</u> use of my <u>hand</u> by next week. <u>No mistake</u>
                        A   B   C   D

22 She is a <u>member</u> of several <u>charitable</u> <u>organizeations</u>. <u>No mistake</u>
                       F   G   H   J

23 It is <u>difficult</u> to solve such a <u>complicatted</u> <u>problem</u>. <u>No mistake</u>
                  A   B   C   D

24 Sara went to the <u>hospital</u> to <u>deliver</u> Joel's <u>simpathy</u> card. <u>No mistake</u>
                                F   G   H   J

25 That was the <u>drearyest</u> <u>meeting</u> I have ever <u>attended</u>. <u>No mistake</u>
                             A   B   C   D

26 She has <u>strong</u> <u>memories</u> of her early <u>childhood</u>. <u>No mistake</u>
                     F   G   H   J

UNIT NINE
Practice Test 1

Reading Comprehension

Sample A

Polar Bears

Polar bears are sometimes called ice bears or snow bears. These huge bears live in the icy lands near the North Pole. They sometimes weigh more than 1,000 pounds. Polar bears live by themselves except when a mother has cubs. Their thick, white fur and layers of fat help them stay warm in freezing winters.

Why can polar bears live near the North Pole?

A They build fires.

B They huddle close together.

C They stay in caves all winter.

D They have thick fur and layers of fat.

For questions 1–30, carefully read each selection and the questions that follow. Then darken the circle for the correct answer to each question, or write in the answer.

Neon Lights

Have you seen brightly colored lights flashing in front of restaurants and other businesses? These brightly colored lights are most likely made from a gas called neon. Neon is one of many gases in the earth's atmosphere. About eighty years ago, Georges Claude, a French chemist, found a way to use neon to make lights. He took the air out of a glass tube and replaced it with neon. When electricity was passed through the neon, a colorful light was created.

You have probably seen neon lights in restaurant signs or on highways. Airports sometimes use neon lights to guide airplanes because neon can be seen through thick fog. Some people use neon signs in their businesses and offices. Some pieces of art are made of neon lights.

1 Why did the author begin with a question ?

A to explain the meaning of "neon"

B to outline and summarize the main ideas in the article

C to show that the topic relates to the reader's experience

D to identify the main character

2 Neon lights are used at airports because

_____

_____

3 This article was mainly written to—

F describe the various kinds of neon signs.

G describe the advantages of neon lights.

H advertise neon lights.

J inform us about neon.

4 What is neon?

A a gas used to make signs

B a brightly colored sign

C a kind of electricity

D a thick fog

95

STATE SWIMMING FINALS
WESTMONT HIGH SCHOOL
JUNE 22

Welcome to the 100th Annual State Swimming Finals for the state of Iowa. We are happy to report that each high school in the state is represented in the meet this year. Swimmers who are participating have qualified for these events during school competitions. Good luck to one and all!

BOYS' EVENTS	
9:00 A.M. 100-, 200-, 800-, 1,500-meter Freestyle	Swimmers may choose any stroke. Most use the front crawl, which is usually the fastest stroke.
10:00 A.M. 400-meter Freestyle Relay	Four swimmers make up a team. Each team member swims 100 meters. The team with the lowest combined time wins.
10:30 A.M. 800-meter Freestyle Medley	Four swimmers make up a team. Each team member swims a different stroke for 200 meters. The team with the lowest combined time wins.
11:00 A.M. 100-meter, 200-meter Butterfly	Come watch the most graceful stroke performed in swimming. The butterfly stroke, when performed correctly, looks like a butterfly in flight.
11:30 A.M. 100-meter, 200-meter Backstroke	The back crawl is another name for the backstroke. The stroke is somewhat similar to the front crawl, except it is performed as the swimmer lies on his back.
12:00 Food sold in the cafeteria.	
GIRLS' EVENTS	
1:00 P.M. 100-, 200-, 400-, 800-meter Freestyle	As in the boys' freestyle event, girls swim using the stroke of their choice.
2:00 P.M. 400-meter Freestyle Relay	Four swimmers make up a team. Each team member swims 100 meters. The team with the lowest combined time wins.
3:00 P.M. 100-meter, 200-meter Butterfly	This popular race looks easy because it is so graceful, but it takes a great deal of endurance.
4:00 P.M. 100-meter, 200-meter Backstroke	Although the backstroke is similar to the front crawl, the backstroke is performed more slowly than the front crawl.

5:00 P.M. Demonstration of Synchronized Swimming—All participating schools have a team of synchronized swimmers, who will demonstrate their graceful, acrobatic movements to music.

5:30 P.M. Medal presentation. The top three winners in each event will be presented with medals.

5 If you leave at 3:30 P.M., you will miss—

  F all the boys' events.

  G the boys' 800-meter freestyle medley.

  H the girls' 100-meter backstroke.

  J all the girls' events.

6 Which of the events listed in the program probably requires the most endurance?

  A 100-meter freestyle

  B 400-meter freestyle relay

  C 200-meter butterfly

  D 200-meter backstroke

7 Which swimmers will take part in the demonstration of synchronized swimming?

  F teams from all participating schools

  G the top three winners in each event

  H the winners of the 800-meter freestyle

  J the swim team from the host school

8 Who will participate in this swim meet and how did they qualify for it?

  _____
  _____
  _____
  _____
  _____
  _____
  _____

9 According to the swim meet program, which event will be performed by the girls, but not the boys?

  A 400-meter freestyle relay

  B 400-meter freestyle

  C 100-meter butterfly

  D 100-meter backstroke

10 There is enough information presented in this program of events to show that—

  F more girls than boys will race in the swim meet.

  G food can be bought in the cafeteria.

  H you will miss a boys' event if you watch a girls' event.

  J most people watch the girls' events.

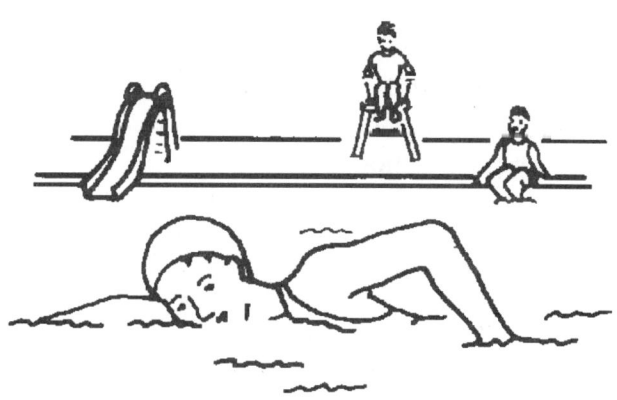

Laura's Summer Project

It was the middle of summer, and Laura was bored. Her best friend was away on vacation, and her brother was at camp. She didn't have anyone to play with or talk to.

She decided to bicycle up the street to the bookstore. She liked to visit there. It had a lot of interesting toys, posters, and computer games, as well as books. She had become friends with Mr. Hoffman, the owner.

"How are you doing today, Laura?" Mr. Hoffman greeted her.

"Okay, I guess. I'm kind of bored," she confessed.

"Well, I have something exciting to show you," he said. "It's about one of your favorite authors." He led her to the notice board. She read the poster.

Laura was so excited she could hardly stand still. She had read all of Elizabeth Blalock's books. Laura thought Ms. Blalock was a wonderful writer. She couldn't think of anything more wonderful than meeting her—except maybe winning the contest and having a story of her own published! Suddenly Laura wasn't bored anymore. "Thanks, Mr. Hoffman!" she said as she hurried out the door.

MEET ELIZABETH BLALOCK

Well-known author Elizabeth Blalock will be at Treehouse Bookstore on Saturday, July 13, from 1:00 P.M. to *autograph* copies of her books.

STORY-WRITING CONTEST

Contest sponsored by Treehouse Bookstore and open to boys and girls ages 6–12.

Contest Rules

Stories must be:
1. Original fiction
2. Between 500 and 700 words in length
3. Neatly written or typed

Mail your story to:
Treehouse Bookstore
1204 Jefferson Avenue
Madison, Wisconsin 53047

We must receive your story by August 1.

Winners will be notified on August 15.

Contest Prizes

First place: $50 Treehouse Bookstore gift certificate
Second and Third places: $30 Treehouse Bookstore gift certificates

Ms. Blalock will judge our story-writing contest and hold a personal writing conference with the first-place winner. Then the winning story will be published in *Tom Thumb* magazine.

11 In this selection, *autograph* means—

 A to illustrate a book.

 B to sign one's name.

 C to give away money.

 D to sell a book.

12 How did Laura feel after she read the poster?

 F She was worried.

 G She was excited and eager to start writing a story.

 H She was still bored.

 J She was sad.

13 Why did Laura like to visit the bookstore?

 A She needed a book for class.

 B It sold birthday cards and balloons.

 C She needed a poster for her bedroom.

 D It had interesting toys, posters, games, and books.

14 Besides the Treehouse Bookstore, where else would you most likely find this poster?

 F at camp

 G at the beach

 H at the library

 J at the post office

15 Why does Laura want to enter the contest?

_____

_____

_____

16 For this contest, you may enter—

 A a story you made up.

 B a report on an animal.

 C a biography about a famous person.

 D a short poem.

17 Where does most of the selection take place?

 F in a bookstore

 G at a camp

 H in a shopping center

 J in a department store

18 Which of these is an *opinion* expressed in the selection?

 A Ms. Blalock writes books.

 B Laura and Mr. Hoffman are friends.

 C Ms. Blalock is a wonderful writer.

 D Laura often goes to the bookstore.

19 Which of these statements is the best summary of the story?

 F Laura was bored because her best friend was away on vacation and her brother was at camp.

 G Laura liked to go to the bookstore and was friends with Mr. Hoffman, the owner.

 H Ms. Blalock will judge a story-writing contest sponsored by Treehouse Bookstore.

 J Laura was bored until she learned that one of her favorite authors would be the judge in a story-writing contest.

GO ON

Navajo Life

The Navajo make up one of the largest groups of Native Americans in the United States. Archaeologists believe that the Navajo used to live in Canada or Alaska. About five hundred years ago, they moved into the region where they now live: Arizona, New Mexico, and Utah.

Navajo spiritual beliefs were centered around their homeland. They believed that the four mountains that defined their territory were sacred. Often, members of the group made long, difficult journeys to the four mountains and collected soil from the top of each. The four bits of soil were wrapped in a small pouch. This became the individual's sacred bundle and was treasured throughout the person's life. Stories about the beginning of the world explained physical features in the region. For example, black lava near Grants, New Mexico, is thought to be the dried blood of a monster that was killed by a Navajo hero.

Traditionally the Navajo lived in hogans—dome-shaped shelters covered with earth. Doorways faced east to greet the sun. The Navajo did not live in villages, but sometimes they situated their hogans near those of relatives. A small settlement might include a few hogans, a herd of sheep, grazing land, and some fields where corn and other vegetables were grown. Marriages were often arranged between families. Girls were usually married at an early age, and the couple lived near the girl's mother. The girl's mother was the head of the household and ruled over the family group.

Every Navajo belongs to one of about sixty clans. Clans are groups of relatives who share a belief that they have a common ancestor. Salt People, Bitter Water, Many Goats, and Water Flowing Together are the names of a few clans. Two people from the same clan may not marry.

Since the late 1700s, sheep have played an important role in traditional Navajo life. The sheep are owned by individuals but graze in one big herd. Parents give lambs to their children so that they can learn to take care of them. Sheep are also an important source of meat. Both lamb and mutton are eaten. Mutton is often cooked with vegetables to make a stew.

Once a year the sheep are sheared. Women weave the wool into blankets with bold, colorful designs. The blankets are greatly admired by people outside the group and to this day continue to be sold or traded for other items. Navajo craft workers also have become well known for the turquoise jewelry they make.

Although a number of Navajo are sheep ranchers or farmers, many are technicians, teachers, miners, and engineers. The growth of industry on Navajo land makes these Native Americans one of the richest groups in the country. Each year the Navajo earn millions of dollars from mining operations. The Navajo also own a lumber mill and a manufacturing plant, which they lease to an electronics firm. In addition, the first college owned and operated by Native Americans, Navajo Community College, is located on Navajo land.

The Navajo gained fame during World War II. The Allies needed a secret code that the Japanese could not break. The son of a missionary, who had grown up on Navajo land, suggested that the Navajo language be used for the code. The Marines liked the idea and recruited hundreds of Navajo to train as Codetalkers. The Codetalkers were able to communicate rapidly, and the code was never broken by the Japanese.

20 A sacred bundle contains—

　A　turquoise and silver collected from the mines.

　B　soil collected from the four holy mountains.

　C　black lava and ash.

　D　feathers and polished stones.

21 Which of these is a *fact* stated in this selection?

　F　People from different clans do not associate.

　G　The journeys to the four mountains were long and difficult.

　H　Many Goats is the most unusual name of a Navajo clan.

　J　Sheep play the most important role in Navajo life.

22 The growth of industry on Navajo land has probably—

　A　brought increased poverty to the Navajo.

　B　caused many Navajo to look for work away from Navajo land.

　C　helped the Navajo become more self-sufficient.

　D　led to a decline in the Navajo population.

23 How do the Navajo explain some of the physical features of their homeland?

　F　They talk about geology.

　G　They have stories about the beginning of the world to explain these features.

　H　They believe that other Native Americans formed the land.

　J　They accept the world and do not try to explain it.

24 According to the selection, where do most Navajo live?

_____

_____

_____

_____

_____

_____

25 The web shows some ideas discussed in the selection.

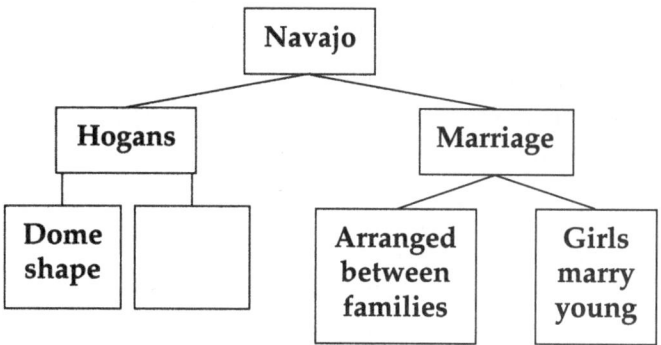

Which of these belongs in the empty box?

　A　Difficult journeys

　B　Electronics firm

　C　Covered with earth

　D　Weave into blankets

26 There is enough information in this article to show that—

　F　the Navajo made an important contribution to the Allies in World War II.

　G　Navajo crafts are greatly valued, but no longer handmade.

　H　buffalo played an important role in traditional Navajo life.

　J　today there are many Navajo in the United States Marines.

Jerry's Plan

The other day while my family and I were stuck in a traffic jam, my brother Jerry started to draw what he called the "future vehicle." It was the most unusual vehicle I had ever seen.

We had just heard a siren. It was an ambulance trying to make its way through the thick traffic jam on the highway. It had to zigzag through the slow-moving automobiles.

"You see, that's the problem with ambulances. They are too wide to navigate easily through heavy traffic. They should be *elongated* and narrower. Then they could fit between lanes of traffic. Look at my idea of an ambulance," said Jerry, pointing to his unearthly drawing.

As traffic began to flow smoothly, Jerry continued to explain how his version of an ambulance would work. It was beginning to make sense to me. Dad said it was a great idea. Mom suggested that Jerry get a patent for his invention to make sure his idea was not stolen.

Jerry was excited and decided to find out how to get a patent. He went to the library and read about patents. Jerry learned that before you try to obtain a patent for your idea, you must make sure that no one has a similar patent already. Some people hire an agent to check this for them. The agent checks with the U.S. Patent and Trademark Office, which has millions of patents registered. The agent must also check foreign patents. After the search, Jerry would have to fill out an application and include drawings and a description of his new vehicle. It could take as long as two years for the patent to be granted.

If Jerry receives his patent, he will be given a patent number that tells the date of the invention. Jerry will have certain rights as an inventor. No one other than the inventor can make or sell the patented item for 17 years.

Learning about patents was an interesting experience. Jerry learned that he is not the only one with an unusual invention. I hope that his idea is successful and that it does not become just another number on the shelf in the U.S. Patent and Trademark Office in Arlington, Virginia.

---

27 The boxes below show events from the selection.

Jerry observed an ambulance stuck in a traffic jam.		Dad said Jerry's new ambulance was a great idea.
1	2	3

Which event belongs in the second box?

A Jerry went to the library.

B Jerry drew the "future vehicle."

C Jerry learned about the patent process.

D Mom suggested Jerry get a patent.

28 Why does Jerry think ambulances should be narrower?

F They could be seen more easily.

G They could fit between traffic lanes.

H They could move more quickly.

J They would prevent traffic jams.

29 In this selection, *elongated* means—

A broken into parts.

B lengthened.

C removed.

D trimmed.

30 What conclusion can be drawn from the last sentence of the selection?

_____
_____
_____
_____
_____
_____

UNIT TEN
Practice Test 2

Reading Vocabulary

Sample A

To adapt is to—

A take
B borrow
C adjust
D run

For questions 1–9, darken the circle for the word or group of words that has the same or almost the same meaning as the underlined word.

1 Frigid means—

A warm
B tight
C stiff
D cold

2 Something that is definite is—

F certain
G sweet
H harmful
J important

3 Gradual means—

A back and forth
B one by one
C little by little
D over and over

4 Someone who is courteous is—

F polite
G rude
H stern
J happy

5 A person who is valiant is—

A meek
B wealthy
C weak
D courageous

6 A petition is a kind of—

F charity
G request
H poison
J conference

7 A cunning person is—

A popular
B sly
C educated
D well known

8 If you dispose of something, you—

F wash it
G paint it
H throw it away
J cover it

9 Another word that means the same thing as reinforced is—

A purchased
B strengthened
C burned
D emptied

Sample B

> Those beams will support the roof.

In which sentence does support have the same meaning as it does in the sentence above?

A That planet cannot support life.

B He thanked us for our support during the campaign.

C That table will not support this heavy lamp.

D The oldest child helped support the family.

For questions 10–14, darken the circle for the sentence in which the underlined word means the same as it does in the sentence in the box.

10
> She offered no excuse for her mistake.

In which sentence does excuse have the same meaning as it does in the sentence above?

F The judge will excuse her from jury duty.

G We'll excuse the noise from outside.

H What is her excuse for missing class?

J Please excuse me for a moment.

11
> I lost my ring near the tennis net.

In which sentence does net have the same meaning as it does in the sentence above?

A She will net the fish.

B The net weight of this box of cereal is 13 ounces.

C Grandmother Lucy always wears a hair net to bed.

D He hopes to net great profits from these investments.

12
> Mom is cleaning the window frame.

In which sentence does frame have the same meaning as it does in the sentence above?

F My uncle has a very large frame.

G I bowled a strike in the first frame of the game.

H Please frame your questions carefully.

J I need a new frame for this picture.

13
> They range in size from small to extra large.

In which sentence does range have the same meaning as it does in the sentence above?

A The plane flew out of radar range.

B The prices range from two dollars to ten dollars.

C My aunt camped in that mountain range during her vacation last year.

D A pot of soup simmered on the range.

14
> Don't force the child to eat.

In which sentence does force have the same meaning as it does in the sentence above?

F Will the storm force us to cancel our plans to go camping?

G Is this school rule still in force?

H Electricity is a powerful force.

J The sales force was given a bonus for their outstanding work this year.

Sample C

The king issued a proclamation stating that everyone in the kingdom had to pay the new tax. Proclamation means—

A report.
B law.
C announcement.
D letter.

For questions 15–21, darken the circle for the word or words that give the meaning of the underlined word, or write in the answer.

15 Please secure this rope to the dock. Secure means—

A fasten.
B paint.
C measure.
D throw.

16 Ling was very excited to get her favorite star's autograph. Autograph means—

F photograph.
G address.
H telephone number.
J signature.

17 Robin Hood is a famous fictitious character. Fictitious means—

A heroic.
B imaginary.
C adventurous.
D real.

18 This puppy is apparently lost. Apparently means—

F always.
G hardly.
H slightly.
J clearly.

19 The police assured her that it was merely a routine investigation. Routine means—

A short.
B serious.
C regular.
D private.

20 The guide told us to heed his instructions so we would not get lost in the forest. Heed means—

F mind.
G ignore.
H read.
J sing.

21 We had to walk seven miles from the plane to the remote mountain village. What is meant by remote?

_____
_____
_____
_____

105

UNIT ELEVEN
Practice Test 3

Part 1: Math Problem Solving

Sample A

What number is shown here?

60,000 + 5,000 + 10 + 8

A 60,518
B 65,018
C 605,108
D 650,018

For questions 1–53, darken the circle for the correct answer, or write in the answer.

1 It is 38.459 meters from the reviewer's stand to the end of the parade route. What is the value of the 4 in this number?

  A 4 hundred-thousandths
  B 4 thousandths
  C 4 hundredths
  D 4 tenths

2 Jan is making a quilt. The pattern requires these fabrics and amounts.

Blue floral	$1\frac{7}{8}$ yds.
White solid	$2\frac{1}{8}$ yds.
Gold checked	$2\frac{2}{3}$ yds.
Navy calico	$2\frac{1}{4}$ yds.

Jan uses the *most* of which fabric?

  F Blue floral
  G White solid
  H Gold checked
  J Navy calico

3 What fraction means the same as $\frac{38}{6}$?

  A $6\frac{1}{6}$
  B $6\frac{1}{3}$
  C $6\frac{3}{6}$
  D $6\frac{7}{6}$

4 Each square represents 0.01. What decimal number is shown below?

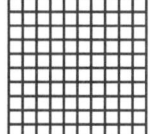 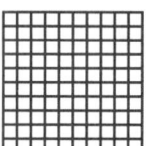 

  F 0.239
  G 2.0239
  H 2.39
  J 23.9

5 What mixed number is shown by the shaded part of the circles?

  A $\frac{6}{8}$
  B $1\frac{3}{4}$
  C $1\frac{2}{6}$
  D $1\frac{2}{6}$

 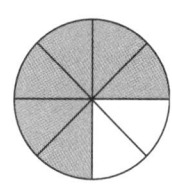

6 There are 34,578 permanent seats at the outdoor concert arena. In addition, there are 1,000 temporary seats set up for the concert. How many seats are there altogether?

  F 33,578
  G 34,478
  H 34,678
  J 35,578

7 Mr. Campos raises turkeys. To measure their growth, he records their weights periodically. Yesterday he weighed a turkey at 4.63 kilograms, another at 4.7 kilograms, a third at 4.09 kilograms, and a fourth at 4.04 kilograms. List the weights of the turkeys in order from lightest to heaviest.

_____

_____

8 If $\frac{9}{13} - x = \frac{9}{13}$, then $x =$

_____

_____

_____

9 If $130 + x = 420$, what number replaces the x to make the sentence true?

A 550

B 390

C 290

D 210

10 Each section of the parking garage has 4 levels and each level has 45 parking spaces. Which number sentence shows how to find T, the total number of parking spaces in 6 sections of the garage?

F $(4 \times 6) \div T = 45$

G $(4 \times 45) \times 6 = T$

H $(4 \times T) \times 6 = 45$

J $(4 \times 45) \div 6 = T$

11 These beads represent the number 351,642,227. What place value is represented by the wire with 6 beads?

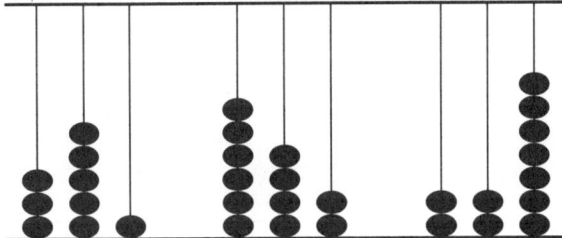

A hundred millions

B ten millions

C millions

D hundred thousands

12 What is the smallest number of raffle tickets that can be shared equally among 6 children with no tickets left over or among 18 children with no tickets left over?

F 36

G 24

H 18

J 8

13 Which of the these number sentences is related to $28 \div 4 = \square$?

A $4 \times \square = 28$

B $28 - 4 = \square$

C $4 + \square = 28$

D $28 + 4 = \square$

14 The Lakewood High School Chess Club held their annual fall bake sale last week to raise funds for new chess sets. They made a total of 173 items to sell. They sold 57 cakes and 103 cookies. What number sentence could be used to find L, the number of baked goods left unsold?

F $173 - (57 + 103) = L$

G $57 + L = 173 + 103$

H $173 + (103 - 57) = L$

J $L - (57 \times 103) - 173$

15 Cassie has 24 cartoon videos, 4 family videos, and 12 movie videos. If she randomly selects 1 video off the shelf, what is the probability that it will be a cartoon?

A $\frac{1}{24}$
B $\frac{1}{6}$
C $\frac{1}{2}$
D $\frac{3}{5}$

16 It is Oliver's turn in a board game he is playing with his cousins. What is the probability that Oliver will have to go back 2 spaces on this spin?

F $\frac{1}{4}$
G $\frac{1}{8}$
H $\frac{3}{8}$
J $\frac{5}{8}$

17 Which vowel (a, e, i, o, u) appears most frequently in the following sentence?

The elephants graze near the mountains.

A a
B e
C i
D u

18 Tomás has 6 nickels and 8 pennies in his backpack. What is the probability that Tomás will randomly pick a nickel out of his backpack?

F $\frac{1}{8}$
G $\frac{1}{6}$
H $\frac{3}{7}$
J $\frac{5}{3}$

19 Cards labeled with A, B, C, or D are placed on a table. What is the probability of choosing a card with the letter C?

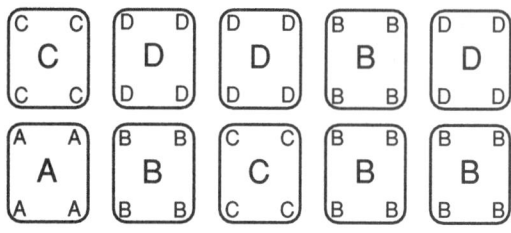

A $\frac{1}{10}$
B $\frac{1}{5}$
C $\frac{1}{4}$
D $\frac{1}{2}$

20 Nielson's Sporting Goods Store sells polo tops with short sleeves or long sleeves. They come in white, red, and black. They come in small, medium, and large. How many total choices of polo tops are there?

_____
_____
_____
_____
_____
_____

This graph shows the results of a survey regarding trips people make. Use the graph to answer questions 21 and 22.

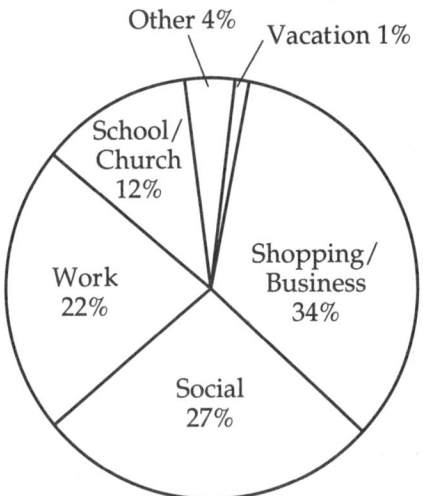

Trips People Make

21 Which two categories account for most of the trips people make?

F School/Church and Vacation

G Shopping/Business and Social

H Social and Work

J Work and Shopping/Business

22 Out of 100 trips, how many are made for shopping/business reasons?

A 4

B 12

C 22

D 34

23 Wanda is trying to decide what to wear to school. On this particular morning, she has 3 pairs of jeans, 4 tops, and 2 pairs of shoes to choose from. How many different clothing combinations does Wanda have?

F 24

G 14

H 12

J 9

24 A special machine multiplies any number entered into it by a secret number. The table below shows how the numbers are changed. Which numbers complete the table?

Original number	5	8	9
New number	35		

A 40 and 43

B 44 and 72

C 40 and 63

D 56 and 63

25 There are 4 red beads, 8 yellow beads, and 2 pink beads in a container. If 1 bead is picked at random from the container, what are the chances that it will be red?

_____

_____

_____

_____

26 Which line segment names a radius of the circle shown here?

F $\overline{AC}$
G $\overline{AB}$
H $\overline{PB}$
J $\overline{CA}$

27 The graph shown here is a record of Karen's growth. Approximately how many inches did Karen grow between the ages of 6 and 9?

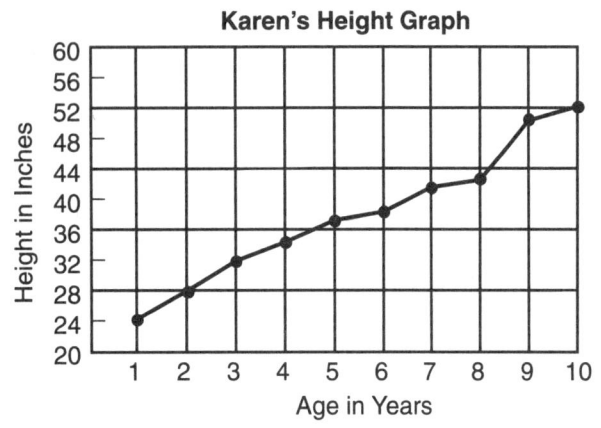

_____
_____

28 What kind of angle is formed by the hands of the clock?

A less than 90°
B exactly 90°
C exactly 180°
D more than 90° and less than 180°

This table shows the total reading time for Mr. Rivera's 8 honor students for each week of March. Use the table to answer questions 29 and 30.

Weekly Reading	
Week	Hours
1	14
2	18
3	16
4	12

29 What was the average number of hours per week in March that the students spent reading?

F 15 hours
G 14 hours
H 13 hours
J 12 hours

30 Which tally chart shows the information presented in the table?

A
Week 1									
Week 2													I
Week 3									III
Week 4									II

B
Week 1									IIII
Week 2									II
Week 3													III
Week 4													

C
Week 1													
Week 2									II
Week 3													I
Week 4													III

D
Week 1									IIII
Week 2													III
Week 3													I
Week 4									II

31 What is the area of the shaded section of this figure?

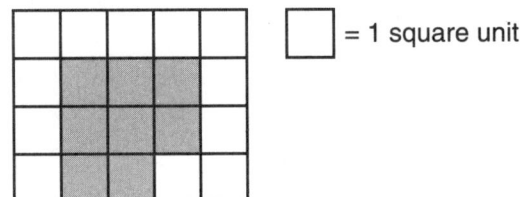

F 20 square units

G 12 square units

H 9 square units

J 8 square units

32 Which figure shows a translation of the car?

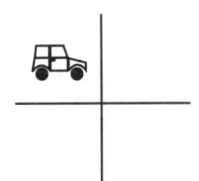

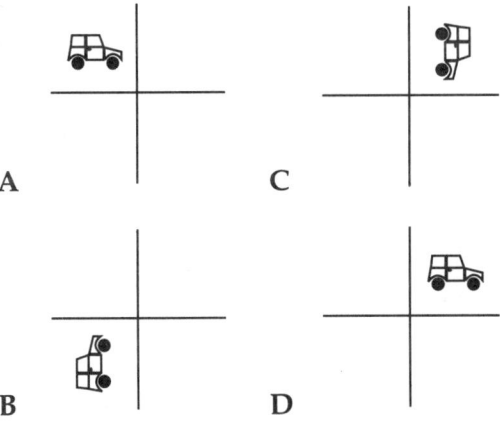

33 Which of the following metric units of measurement is best to use to measure the capacity of a bucket?

F centimeter

G liter

H kilograms

J milligram

34 Ray bought the toys shown below at the toy store. Which of the toys has a line of symmetry?

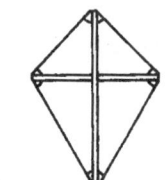

A

B

C

D

35 Name the coordinates of point B shown on the grid.

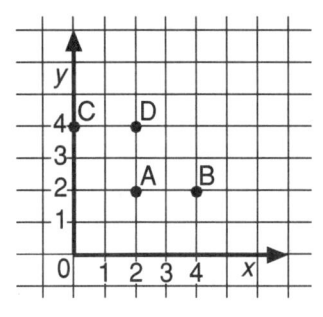

36. A musical program began at 4:05 P.M. If it lasted 1 hour and 30 minutes, at what time did the program end?

   F 5:35 P.M.   H 6:05 P.M.
   G 5:50 P.M   J 6:40 P.M.

37. Use your inch ruler and the map to help you answer the question. What is the actual distance between the two farms?

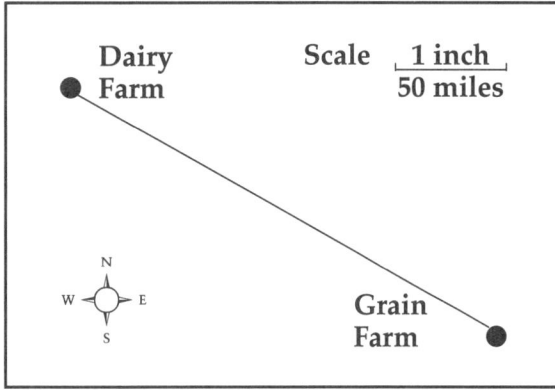

   A 200 miles   C 125 miles
   B 175 miles   D 75 miles

38. Use your inch ruler to help you answer this question. How would you calculate the perimeter of this miniature magnetic frame?

39. Katie measured a piece of rope 18 feet long. How many yards is that?

   F 648 yd   H 6 yd
   G 54 yd   J $\frac{1}{2}$ yd

40. Which shaded shape shown here has an area of 11 square units?

   □ = 1 square unit

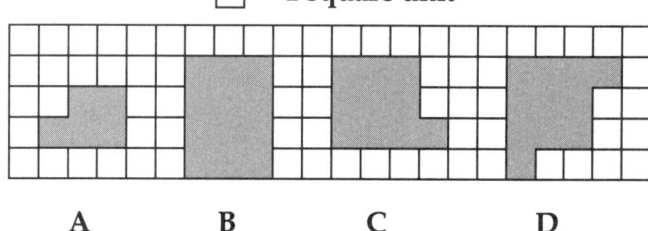

   A   B   C   D

41. Use your centimeter ruler to help you answer this question. Which figure shown here has an area of 5cm²?

   F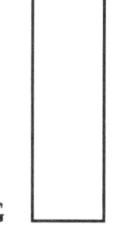

   G

   H

   J

112

42 Lisa measured 8 gallons of water. How many quarts is that?

A 128 quarts

B 32 quarts

C 16 quarts

D 2 quarts

43 The school store sells paper with or without binder holes that is available in white or yellow. The paper comes in 3 sizes. How many choices of paper do students have when buying paper at the school store?

F 12

G 7

H 6

J 3

44 Which shows the piece that is missing from the figure?

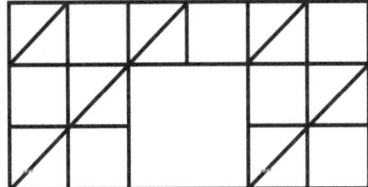

A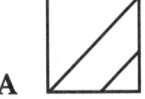

B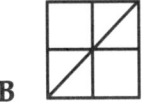

C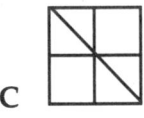

D

45 Kala is a photographer who sells her portraits for $46.95 each. Last week she sold 8 portraits. What is the best estimate for Kala's total earnings for the portraits?

F $200

G $300

H $400

J $500

46 Marco designed the rock wall around his garden by using 2 brown rocks, then 5 gray rocks, then 8 tan rocks, then 3 white rocks. If Marco continues this pattern, what will be the color of the thirty-fifth rock?

A white

B tan

C gray

D brown

47 Stephanie is 5 inches taller than her cousin. What other information is needed to find the height of Stephanie's cousin?

48 The sum of the first two numerals in Max's apartment number is twice the sum of the last two numerals. Which of these could be Max's apartment number?

   F 842
   G 824
   H 428
   J 248

49 Each rectangular prism in the picture is equal in weight to 2 cylinders. What should be added to Side A in order to balance the scales?

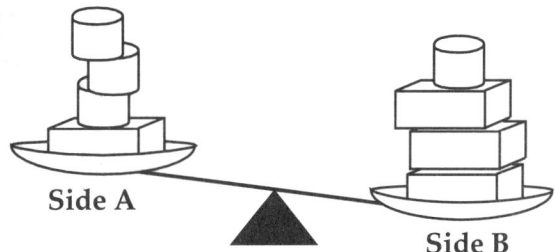

   A 1 cylinder
   B 2 cylinders
   C 1 rectangular prism and 1 cylinder
   D 2 rectangular prisms

50 Karen, Bill, and Mike turned in the most book reports during the first grading period. Mike did not read the most and Karen did not read the least. Bill had fewer book reports than Mike. Which of these shows the order from most to the least number of book reports?

   F Karen, Bill, Mike
   G Mike, Bill, Karen
   H Karen, Mike, Bill
   J Bill, Mike, Karen

51 David went shopping for school clothes. He bought 2 pairs of slacks, 3 shirts, and 1 sweater. What do you *not* need to know to find out how much money David had left after shopping?

   A how many hours David shopped
   B how much money David started with
   C how much money each pair of slacks cost
   D how much money the sweater cost

52 There are 13 dancers in one chorus line and 29 dancers in another chorus line. How many dancers need to move from the second line to the first line in order to have the same number of dancers in both chorus lines?

   F 24
   G 16
   H 8
   J 4

53 The Hernandez family raised 558 cattle. They sold 215 of them. What is the best estimate of the number of cattle they have left?

Part 2: Math Procedures

Sample A

$8 \times 0.6 =$

A 0.0048
B 0.48
C 1.4
D 4.8
E NH

Sample B

Susan had $2\frac{5}{6}$ pizzas left from her party. What is that amount rounded to the nearest whole number?

F $2\frac{1}{2}$
G 3
H 4
J 5
K NH

STOP

Directions: For questions 1–13, darken the circle for the correct answer, or write in the answer. Darken the circle for *NH, Not Here,* if the correct answer is not given.

1

$58 \times 24 =$

A 348
B 1,126
C 1,262
D 1,392
E NH

2

$4\frac{5}{8}$
$-\frac{3}{8}$

F $\frac{2}{8}$
G $4\frac{1}{8}$
H $4\frac{1}{4}$
J $4\frac{1}{2}$
K NH

3

$0.543 + 0.791 =$

A 1.23
B 1.334
C 1.34
D 13.34
E NH

4

$\frac{6}{8}$
$-\frac{1}{2}$

F $\frac{1}{4}$
G $\frac{7}{16}$
H $\frac{3}{8}$
J $\frac{5}{6}$
K NH

5

$\frac{2}{3} \times \frac{4}{5} =$

A $\frac{3}{4}$
B $\frac{8}{15}$
C $\frac{6}{15}$
D $\frac{2}{15}$
E NH

6

$\frac{2}{3}$
$+\frac{3}{10}$

F $\frac{9}{20}$
G $\frac{6}{10}$
H $\frac{7}{10}$
J $\frac{3}{5}$
K NH

7

$675 \div 6 =$

A 110
B 110 R6
C 112
D 112 R3
E NH

GO ON

115

8 Find the product.

   876 × 65 =

   _____
   _____
   _____
   _____

9 Elizabeth wrapped 15 gifts for a grab bag booth at the carnival.

   She needs 5 feet of ribbon for each gift. How many feet of ribbon does she need altogether?

   F 3
   G 10
   H 20
   J 75
   K NH

10 Each admission ticket to the amusement park costs $24.50. A family packet of 5 tickets cost $98.00.

   How much can be saved on 5 tickets by buying the family packet?

   A $3.75
   B $5.50
   C $19.25
   D $24.50
   E NH

11 Alice read 2 books last weekend. She read the first book in $4\frac{3}{4}$ hours and the second book in $3\frac{3}{4}$ hours.

   How many hours did it take Alice to read both books?

   F $8\frac{1}{2}$ hours
   G $7\frac{1}{2}$ hours
   H $6\frac{3}{4}$ hours
   J 1 hour
   K NH

12. Roberto needs to know the net weight of the package he is mailing in order to calculate the amount of postage he will pay.

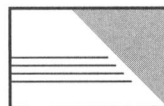

If the package contains 12 copies of a report that weighs 37.3 grams each, what is the total weight of the package?

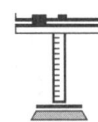

A 447.6 grams

B 424.7 grams

C 398.7 grams

D 49.3 grams

E NH

13. Brian bought 3 boxes of hamster food at the pet store.

Each box cost $ 0.75.

How much change will he get from a ten-dollar bill?

F $8.75

G $7.75

H $6.75

J $2.25

K NH

UNIT TWELVE
Practice Test 4

Listening

Sample A
- A beauty
- B weather
- C conflict
- D hunger

For questions 1–17, darken the circle for the word or words that best complete the sentence you hear.

1
- A cup
- B bottle
- C rope
- D barrel

2
- F withhold
- G explain
- H ask
- J inform

3
- A afterwards
- B later
- C in advance
- D at that time

4
- F dangerous
- G stable
- H secure
- J obvious

5
- A bony
- B fat
- C handsome
- D bearded

6
- F purchase it
- G sell it
- H destroy it
- J change it

7
- A ship
- B sailor
- C storm
- D warning

8
- F coat
- G wagon
- H ship
- J container

9
- A win
- B race
- C try
- D leap

10
- F solve
- G interfere
- H listen
- J ignore

11
- A old
- B bare
- C large
- D dark

12
- F conceited
- G cheerful
- H talented
- J lonely

13
- A work
- B roam
- C hunt
- D journey

14
- F foreign
- G quiet
- H honest
- J unfriendly

15
- A mild
- B pleasant
- C severe
- D dry

16
- F worry
- G discuss
- H think
- J write

17
- A result
- B cause
- C reward
- D description

Sample B

    A corn   C animals

    B insects   D plants

For questions 18–31, listen to the story. Then darken the circle for the word or words that best answer the question.

18   F in a cabin
        G at home
        H in a motel
        J at a friend's house

19   A in their back yard
        B in the woods
        C on a farm
        D in another state

20   F are too high to reach
        G don't have many apples
        H scratch his skin
        J have the most apples

21   A furniture   C dishes
        B jewelry   D decorations

22   F jewelry   H money
        G plate   J food

23   A "Shells Have Many Uses"
        B "Native-American Customs"
        C "Jewelry-Making"
        D "Decorating Your Home with Shells"

24   F "Preparing Your Food"
        G "Setting a Proper Table"
        H "Ways to Cut Preparation Time"
        J "Making Food Tastier"

25   A food magazine
        B news magazine
        C newspaper
        D science book

26   F to the right of each plate
        G at the tip of the knife
        H to the right of the knife
        J to the left of each plate

27   A to the left of each plate
        B at the tip of each knife
        C beside each fork
        D at the tip of each fork

28   F bought basketballs
        G held a bake sale
        H held a meeting
        J cleaned a local playground

29   A a day   C a month
        B a weekend D all year

30   F basketball team
        G student council
        H safety patrol
        J band

31   A They had a bake sale.
        B They had a meeting at the beginning of the school year.
        C They collected money at the playground.
        D They cleaned the playground.

UNIT THIRTEEN
Practice Test 5

Language

Sample A

Nan would like to build a dog exercise pen in her back yard. She saw an exercise pen that she liked in a photograph in the newspaper. Nan decides to write a letter to the newspaper editor asking for information about the pen. Before Nan writes the letter, she needs to find the address of the newspaper. She should look in—

A a thesaurus.
B a telephone book.
C an atlas.
D a dictionary.

For questions 1–4, read the passage below. Then darken the circle for the correct answer to each question, or write in the answer.

Tropical Fish

Andrew has had an aquarium of tropical fish for as long as he can remember. He decided that the care of tropical fish would be an excellent subject for a science research report.

1 Andrew located the book *Tropical Fish: A Complete Pet Owner's Manual.* Where should he look to find the name of the author of the book?

A the table of contents
B the glossary
C the index
D the title page

2 What information would Andrew not want to include in his report?

F a list of the most popular species of tropical fish for aquariums
G a description of the feeding habits of tropical fish
H a discussion of the kinds of tropical fish that can coexist in an aquarium
J a chapter on raising turtles in aquariums

3 What should Andrew do before he writes his report?

_____
_____
_____

4 Which of the following sources should Andrew use to locate a book about tropical fish?

A a telephone directory
B a library card catalog
C a science textbook
D an atlas

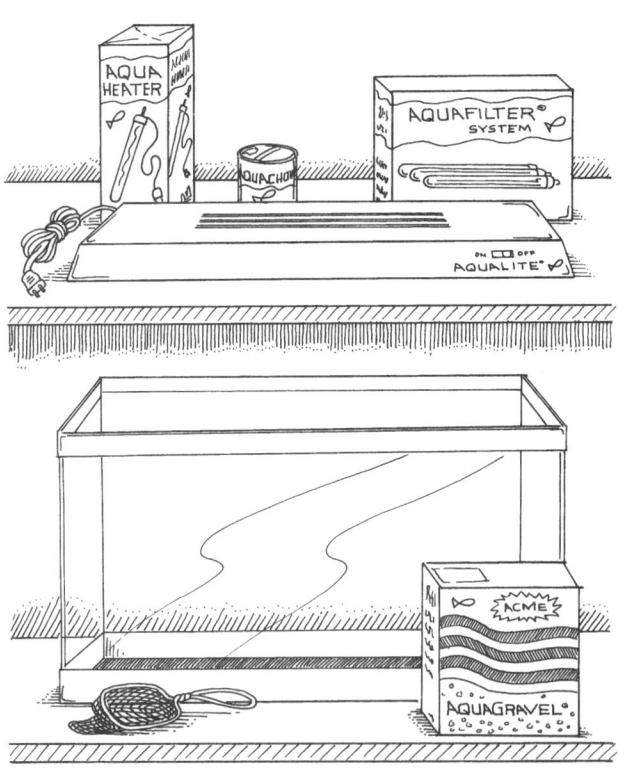

120

Andrew used the dictionary to check some words he wanted to use in his report.

5 Which guide words might mark the page where Andrew would find the word *degree*?

   F definition–degrade
   G delay–desert
   H defeat–defrost
   J deform–delicious

6 What is the correct way to divide <u>thermostat</u> into syllables?

   A ther mos tat
   B therm o stat
   C ther mo stat
   D the rmos tat

Here is the Table of Contents from *Tropical Fish: A Complete Pet Owner's Manual*. Study it carefully. Then answer questions 7 and 8.

Table of Contents
Chapter .... Page
1 How To Choose an Aquarium 5
2 Equipment and Accessories 11
3 Preparing the Aquarium 16
4 Decorating the Aquarium 24
5 Choosing Plants................. 27
6 Choosing Fish 32
7 Feeding and Caring for Fish 35

7 Which chapter should Andrew read to find information about the size of the aquarium to purchase?

   F Chapter 1
   G Chapter 2
   H Chapter 6
   J Chapter 7

8 Which chapter should Andrew read to find information about the best kind of lighting to use in an aquarium?

   A Chapter 1
   B Chapter 2
   C Chapter 3
   D Chapter 4

Here is a rough draft of the first part of Andrew's report. Read the rough draft carefully. Then answer questions 9–12.

Raising Tropical Fish

If you want to raise tropical fish, you must decide how much money you
(1)
want to spend. Consider the kind of fish you want. You also need to know
(2) (3)
how many fish you want to raise. Once you have decided these three things,
(4)
you are ready to buy an aquarium.

You will have many questions to ask, so you want to do business with
(5)
someone who knows about tropical fish. Be sure to get a tank that is made
(6)
and constructed of glass and can be used with salt water. The more fish you
(7)
plan to raise, the larger the tank must be. An aquarium cover is a must
(8)
because it keeps the fish in the tank and the dust out. A good cover has
(9)
openings that allow for feeding the fish, for a heater, and for a filter.

The equipment should include a heater, a thermostat, a filter, and a light
(10)
you need for your aquarium. Other recommended items include a fish net,
(11)
plant tongs, and a window washer. A heater is also necessary because tropical
(12)
fish need water that is constant in temperature.

9 Which sentence could begin the second paragraph?

F It is important to buy your aquarium at a well-respected pet store.

G You should not add fish to the tank until the water has reached the correct temperature.

H Some people add decorative rocks to their aquariums.

J Your favorite fish will live a long healthy life.

10 What is the best way to write sentence 10?

A The equipment should include, a heater, a thermostat, a filter, and a light for your aquarium.

B The equipment for your aquarium, needed are a heater, thermostat, filter, and light.

C The equipment for your aquarium should include a heater, a thermostat, a filter, and a light.

D As it is written.

11 Which group of words needlessly repeats an idea?

F …will have many questions to ask…

G …aquarium cover is a must…

H …many choices of sizes and shapes…

J …that is made and constructed of glass…

12 How can sentences 2 and 3 best be combined?

_____
_____
_____
_____

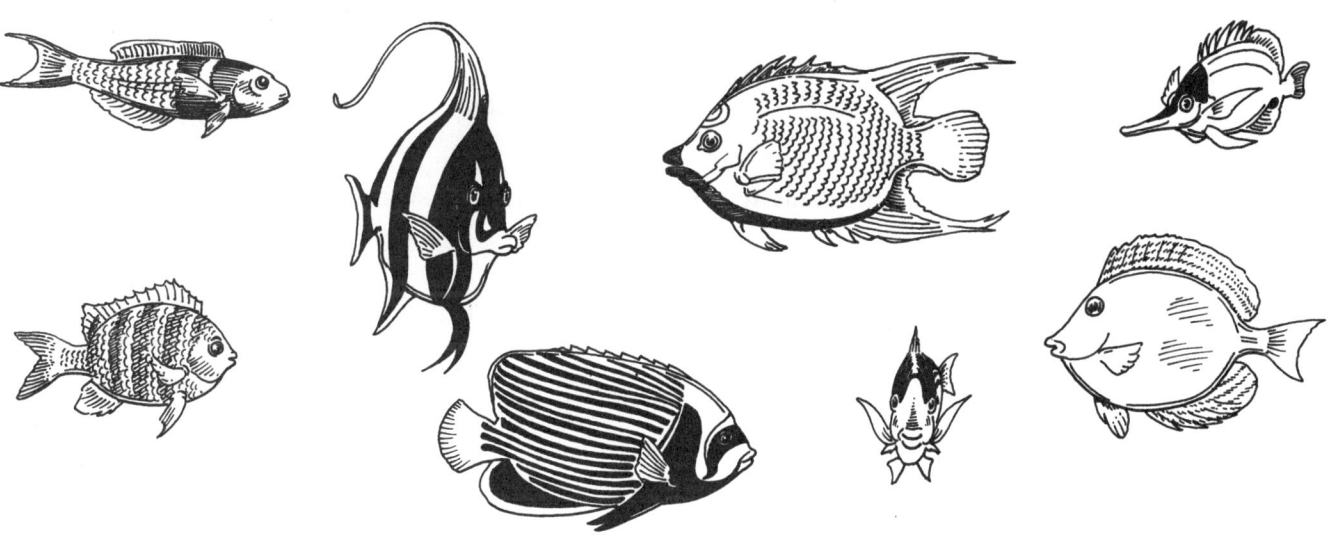

123

Here is the next part of the rough draft of Andrew's report. This part has certain words and phrases underlined. Read the draft carefully. Then answer questions 13–19.

Once you have all <u>you're equipment</u> you are ready to set up the aquarium.
(13)

Place the tank on a level surface and install your filter and heating systems.
(14)

Next, add about 2 inches of gravel or sand to the bottom of the tank. Add
(15) (16)

fertilizer for your plants. It <u>has been found</u> that fertilizer added to the gravel
(17)

or sand helps the plants grow. Add your decorative rocks and driftwood.
(18)

When you <u>are finishing decorating</u> your tank, fill it about one third full
(19)

with water. Be careful not to stir up the gravel. The <u>pet store owner, Ms.
(20) (21)

Lauren Kirby</u> suggests that you place a large plate in the bottom of the tank.

Then slowly pour the water on the plate. Be sure to take the plate out when
(22) (23)

you are finished.

Now you are ready to add your plants. Ms. Kirby <u>suggests, "Make a hole
(24) (25)

in the gravel and place the plant in it as deep as possible. Be sure the root tips
(26)

are pointing down. Arrange the plants so they will be <u>appealing to the eye"</u>.
(27)

<u>Waiting two days</u> before you add your fish to the aquarium. This gives
(28) (29)

the plants a chance to take root.

13 In sentence 13, you're equipment is best written—

A you are equipment
B your equipment
C their equipment
D As it is written.

14 In sentence 17, has been found is best written—

F have found
G has found
H will find
J As it is written.

15 In sentence 19, are finishing decorating is best written—

A is finished decorating
B will be finishing decorating
C have finished decorating
D As it is written.

16 In sentence 21, pet store owner, Ms. Lauren Kirby is best written—

F pet store owner Ms. Lauren Kirby
G pet store owner ms. Lauren Kirby
H pet store owner, Ms. Lauren Kirby,
J As it is written.

17 In sentence 25, suggests, "Make a hole is best written—

A suggests "make a hole
B suggests, "make a hole
C suggests "Make a hole
D As it is written.

18 In sentence 27, appealing to the eye". is best written—

F appealing to the eye."
G appealing to the eye"
H appealing to the eye.
J As it is written.

19 In sentence 28, Waiting two days is best written—

A Waited two days
B Wait two days
C Have waited two days
D As it is written.

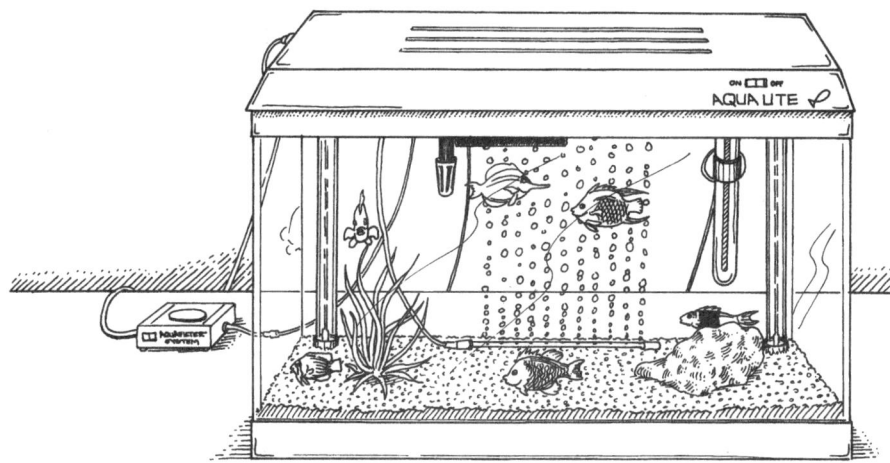

For questions 20–31, read each sentence carefully. If one of the words is misspelled, darken the circle for that word. If all of the words are spelled correctly, darken the circle for *No mistake*.

20 Peter's <u>admireation</u> for his father <u>knows</u> no <u>bounds</u>. <u>No mistake</u>
          F   G   H   J

21 I store my <u>fishing</u> <u>tackle</u> in the <u>garage</u>. <u>No mistake</u>
               A   B   C   D

22 The <u>highway</u> was <u>obstructet</u> by the <u>fallen</u> tree. <u>No mistake</u>
         F   G   H   J

23 Matilda was the <u>stingyest</u> of the three <u>witches</u> in the <u>fable</u>. <u>No mistake</u>
                    A   B   C   D

24 The <u>mechanic</u> lubricated the <u>bearings</u> before he <u>reaplaced</u> them in the wheel. <u>No mistake</u>
         F   G   H   J

25 The Waltons <u>are</u> one of the <u>wealthyest</u> <u>families</u> in the United States. <u>No mistake</u>
                 A   B   C   D

26 Marta <u>addressed</u> the <u>inviteations</u> <u>yesterday</u>. <u>No mistake</u>
           F   G   H   J

27 We <u>always</u> save our <u>receipts</u> for tax <u>purposes</u>. <u>No mistake</u>
        A   B   C   D

28 Xavier is working as a senator's <u>aid</u> during this <u>legislative</u> <u>session</u>. <u>No mistake</u>
                                     F   G   H   J

29 Sammy <u>smearred</u> <u>strawberry</u> jam all over his new <u>shirt</u>. <u>No mistake</u>
           A   B   C   D

30 Mom's new <u>cookware</u> is made of <u>stainless</u> <u>steal</u>. <u>No mistake</u>
               F   G   H   J

31 Miriam <u>honkt</u> her horn at the <u>squirrel</u> in the <u>street</u>. <u>No mistake</u>
            A   B   C   D

Answer Sheet

STUDENT'S NAME — LAST, FIRST, MI

SCHOOL:
TEACHER:
FEMALE ○   MALE ○

BIRTH DATE — MONTH / DAY / YEAR

GRADE ② ③ ④ ⑤ ⑥ ⑦ ⑧

TEST BEST®
FOR TEST PREP

STECK-VAUGHN BERRENT PUBLICATIONS

Fill in the circle for each multiple-choice answer. Write the answers to the open-ended questions on a separate sheet of paper.

TEST 1 — Reading Comprehension

- SA Ⓐ Ⓑ Ⓒ Ⓓ
- 1 Ⓐ Ⓑ Ⓒ Ⓓ
- 2 OPEN ENDED
- 3 Ⓕ Ⓖ Ⓗ Ⓙ
- 4 Ⓐ Ⓑ Ⓒ Ⓓ
- 5 Ⓕ Ⓖ Ⓗ Ⓙ
- 6 Ⓐ Ⓑ Ⓒ Ⓓ
- 7 Ⓕ Ⓖ Ⓗ Ⓙ
- 8 OPEN ENDED
- 9 Ⓐ Ⓑ Ⓒ Ⓓ
- 10 Ⓕ Ⓖ Ⓗ Ⓙ
- 11 Ⓐ Ⓑ Ⓒ Ⓓ
- 12 Ⓕ Ⓖ Ⓗ Ⓙ
- 13 Ⓐ Ⓑ Ⓒ Ⓓ
- 14 Ⓕ Ⓖ Ⓗ Ⓙ
- 15 OPEN ENDED
- 16 Ⓐ Ⓑ Ⓒ Ⓓ
- 17 Ⓕ Ⓖ Ⓗ Ⓙ
- 18 Ⓐ Ⓑ Ⓒ Ⓓ
- 19 Ⓕ Ⓖ Ⓗ Ⓙ
- 20 Ⓐ Ⓑ Ⓒ Ⓓ
- 21 Ⓕ Ⓖ Ⓗ Ⓙ
- 22 Ⓐ Ⓑ Ⓒ Ⓓ
- 23 Ⓕ Ⓖ Ⓗ Ⓙ
- 24 OPEN ENDED
- 25 Ⓐ Ⓑ Ⓒ Ⓓ
- 26 Ⓕ Ⓖ Ⓗ Ⓙ
- 27 Ⓐ Ⓑ Ⓒ Ⓓ
- 28 Ⓕ Ⓖ Ⓗ Ⓙ
- 29 Ⓐ Ⓑ Ⓒ Ⓓ
- 30 OPEN ENDED

TEST 2 — Reading Vocabulary

- SA Ⓐ Ⓑ Ⓒ Ⓓ
- 1 Ⓐ Ⓑ Ⓒ Ⓓ
- 2 Ⓕ Ⓖ Ⓗ Ⓙ
- 3 Ⓐ Ⓑ Ⓒ Ⓓ
- 4 Ⓕ Ⓖ Ⓗ Ⓙ
- 5 Ⓐ Ⓑ Ⓒ Ⓓ
- 6 Ⓕ Ⓖ Ⓗ Ⓙ
- 7 Ⓐ Ⓑ Ⓒ Ⓓ
- 8 Ⓕ Ⓖ Ⓗ Ⓙ
- 9 Ⓐ Ⓑ Ⓒ Ⓓ
- SB Ⓐ Ⓑ Ⓒ Ⓓ
- 10 Ⓕ Ⓖ Ⓗ Ⓙ
- 11 Ⓐ Ⓑ Ⓒ Ⓓ
- 12 Ⓕ Ⓖ Ⓗ Ⓙ
- 13 Ⓐ Ⓑ Ⓒ Ⓓ
- 14 Ⓕ Ⓖ Ⓗ Ⓙ
- SC Ⓐ Ⓑ Ⓒ Ⓓ
- 15 Ⓐ Ⓑ Ⓒ Ⓓ
- 16 Ⓕ Ⓖ Ⓗ Ⓙ
- 17 Ⓐ Ⓑ Ⓒ Ⓓ
- 18 Ⓕ Ⓖ Ⓗ Ⓙ
- 19 Ⓐ Ⓑ Ⓒ Ⓓ
- 20 Ⓕ Ⓖ Ⓗ Ⓙ
- 21 OPEN ENDED

TEST 3 — Part 1: Math Problem Solving

- SA (A) (B) (C) (D)
- 1 (A) (B) (C) (D)
- 2 (F) (G) (H) (J)
- 3 (A) (B) (C) (D)
- 4 (F) (G) (H) (J)
- 5 (A) (B) (C) (D)
- 6 (F) (G) (H) (J)
- 7 Open Ended
- 8 Open Ended
- 9 (A) (B) (C) (D)
- 10 (F) (G) (H) (J)
- 11 (A) (B) (C) (D)
- 12 (F) (G) (H) (J)
- 13 (A) (B) (C) (D)
- 14 (F) (G) (H) (J)
- 15 (A) (B) (C) (D)
- 16 (F) (G) (H) (J)
- 17 (A) (B) (C) (D)
- 18 (F) (G) (H) (J)
- 19 (A) (B) (C) (D)
- 20 Open Ended
- 21 (F) (G) (H) (J)
- 22 (A) (B) (C) (D)
- 23 (F) (G) (H) (J)
- 24 (A) (B) (C) (D)
- 25 Open Ended
- 26 (F) (G) (H) (J)
- 27 Open Ended
- 28 (A) (B) (C) (D)
- 29 (F) (G) (H) (J)
- 30 (A) (B) (C) (D)
- 31 (F) (G) (H) (J)
- 32 (A) (B) (C) (D)
- 33 (F) (G) (H) (J)
- 34 (A) (B) (C) (D)
- 35 Open Ended
- 36 (F) (G) (H) (J)
- 37 (A) (B) (C) (D)
- 38 Open Ended
- 39 (F) (G) (H) (J)
- 40 (A) (B) (C) (D)
- 41 (F) (G) (H) (J)
- 42 (A) (B) (C) (D)
- 43 (F) (G) (H) (J)
- 44 (A) (B) (C) (D)
- 45 (F) (G) (H) (J)
- 46 (A) (B) (C) (D)
- 47 Open Ended
- 48 (F) (G) (H) (J)
- 49 (A) (B) (C) (D)
- 50 (F) (G) (H) (J)
- 51 (A) (B) (C) (D)
- 52 (F) (G) (H) (J)
- 53 Open Ended

Part 2: Math Procedures

- SA (A) (B) (C) (D) (E)
- SB (F) (G) (H) (J) (K)
- 1 (A) (B) (C) (D) (E)
- 2 (F) (G) (H) (J) (K)
- 3 (A) (B) (C) (D) (E)
- 4 (F) (G) (H) (J) (K)
- 5 (A) (B) (C) (D) (E)
- 6 (F) (G) (H) (J) (K)
- 7 (A) (B) (C) (D) (E)
- 8 Open Ended
- 9 (F) (G) (H) (J) (K)
- 10 (A) (B) (C) (D) (E)
- 11 (F) (G) (H) (J) (K)
- 12 (A) (B) (C) (D) (E)
- 13 (F) (G) (H) (J) (K)

TEST 4 — Listening

- SA (A) (B) (C) (D)
- 1 (A) (B) (C) (D)
- 2 (F) (G) (H) (J)
- 3 (A) (B) (C) (D)
- 4 (F) (G) (H) (J)
- 5 (A) (B) (C) (D)
- 6 (F) (G) (H) (J)
- 7 (A) (B) (C) (D)
- 8 (F) (G) (H) (J)
- 9 (A) (B) (C) (D)
- 10 (F) (G) (H) (J)
- 11 (A) (B) (C) (D)
- 12 (F) (G) (H) (J)
- 13 (A) (B) (C) (D)
- 14 (F) (G) (H) (J)
- 15 (A) (B) (C) (D)
- 16 (F) (G) (H) (J)
- 17 (A) (B) (C) (D)
- SB (A) (B) (C) (D)
- 18 (F) (G) (H) (J)
- 19 (A) (B) (C) (D)
- 20 (F) (G) (H) (J)
- 21 (A) (B) (C) (D)
- 22 (F) (G) (H) (J)
- 23 (A) (B) (C) (D)
- 24 (F) (G) (H) (J)
- 25 (A) (B) (C) (D)
- 26 (F) (G) (H) (J)
- 27 (A) (B) (C) (D)
- 28 (F) (G) (H) (J)
- 29 (A) (B) (C) (D)
- 30 (F) (G) (H) (J)
- 31 (A) (B) (C) (D)

TEST 5 — Language

- SA (A) (B) (C) (D)
- 1 (A) (B) (C) (D)
- 2 (F) (G) (H) (J)
- 3 Open Ended
- 4 (A) (B) (C) (D)
- 5 (F) (G) (H) (J)
- 6 (A) (B) (C) (D)
- 7 (F) (G) (H) (J)
- 8 (A) (B) (C) (D)
- 9 (F) (G) (H) (J)
- 10 (A) (B) (C) (D)
- 11 (F) (G) (H) (J)
- 12 Open Ended
- 13 (A) (B) (C) (D)
- 14 (F) (G) (H) (J)
- 15 (A) (B) (C) (D)
- 16 (F) (G) (H) (J)
- 17 (A) (B) (C) (D)
- 18 (F) (G) (H) (J)
- 19 (A) (B) (C) (D)
- 20 (F) (G) (H) (J)
- 21 (A) (B) (C) (D)
- 22 (F) (G) (H) (J)
- 23 (A) (B) (C) (D)
- 24 (F) (G) (H) (J)
- 25 (A) (B) (C) (D)
- 26 (F) (G) (H) (J)
- 27 (A) (B) (C) (D)
- 28 (F) (G) (H) (J)
- 29 (A) (B) (C) (D)
- 30 (F) (G) (H) (J)
- 31 (A) (B) (C) (D)